The South African Truth Commission

The South African Truth Commission
The Politics of Reconciliation

Dorothy C. Shea

UNITED STATES INSTITUTE OF PEACE PRESS

Washington, D.C.

UNITED STATES INSTITUTE OF PEACE
1200 17th Street NW
Washington, DC 20036

First published 2000

Printed in the United States of America

The paper used in this publication meets the minimum requirements of American National Standards for Information Sciences—Permanence of Paper for Printed Library Materials, ANSI Z39.48-1984.

Library of Congress Cataloging-in-Publication Data
Shea, Dorothy C., 1965-
    The South African Truth Commission : the politics of reconciliation / Dorothy C. Shea.
        p. cm.
    Includes bibliographical references (p.).
    ISBN 1-929223-09-9
    1. South Africa. Truth and Reconciliation Commission. 2. South Africa—Politics and government—1989-1994. 3. South Africa—Politics and government—1989- I. Title.

DT1945 .S52 2000
968-06'5—dc21

                                                            00-63452
                                                              CIP

CONTENTS

Foreword *by Charlayne Hunter-Gault*   vii

Preface   xi

1. Introduction   3

2. The Benefits of Learning from Others' Mistakes   9
    Problems with Blanket Amnesty   12
    The Need for Robust Investigatory Powers   16
    The Benefits of a Contextual Approach   19

3. The Politics of the TRC   23
    The Selection of Commissioners   24
    The Politics of the Amnesty Process   26
    The Politics of Reparations (or Not)   33
    The Politics of the Endgame   37
    The Politics of Prosecutions (or Not)   40

4. Report Card   45
    Conceptual Benchmarks   46
    Public Ownership   46
    The Mandate   50
    Impartiality and Independence   52
    Deliverables   55
    Logistical Benchmarks   63
    Administration   63
    Safeguards   67

5. Extrapolating from the TRC   69
    Conducive Environment   69
    Translating Concepts into Practice   73

Conclusion   77

Notes   81

FOREWORD

Shortly after I took up residence in South Africa in 1997, on assignment for National Public Radio, I attended my first session of the Truth and Reconciliation Commission. The commission had been under way for about two years and I was feeling a little bit bypassed by the course of its history. Archbishop Desmond Tutu, the commission's chairman, had already undergone his emotional catharsis months before, collapsing on the table at which he was sitting, his body wracked with sobs after hearing the testimony of a black man in a wheelchair, the victim of torture, harassment, and imprisonment ordered by the apartheid state. And there was more sobbing to come, mostly from other victims of the brutality of the apartheid security agents. "The crying," wrote reporter Antjie Krog, is "the ultimate sound of what the process is all about."

Now, way past all that, I thought, I was entering a room where for the first time top political leaders from the apartheid state were going to testify about their role in what one called "the dirty war" against its opponents. The hearing was supposed to establish a clear picture of the chain of command from top to bottom—to determine who gave the orders that resulted in thousands of atrocities committed by police, soldiers, and freelance terrorists of the state. Up to that point, the testimony of the "little" people—generals, police, and others toward the lower end of the totem poll—had conflicted with the politicians. The operatives had said that they had been authorized by the politicians (up to and including the state president); the political leaders, in their written submissions to the commission, had claimed that they had not.

As I entered the room, I was stunned by the ordinariness of it. I'm not sure what I was expecting, but what I found was a gray, airless room, crowded with journalists and other observers. The commissioners were sitting behind wooden desks at the front of the room, between witnesses on one side and the investigators who were to ask most of the questions on the other. And everyone was just milling around, as if they were waiting for something as ordinary as the room we were in.

Most of the radio journalists were in a separate room, where they could take a "clean" feed of the proceedings directly from the microphones being used by the participants. I busied myself trying to get a seat near the speaker that was amplifying the proceedings in the hearing room. Since this was the first hearing I had attended, I wanted to see the faces and the body language. I also wanted to witness the precise moment, if it occurred, at which the sweat broke out on the face of one pressed by the weight of the proceedings into admitting the truth.

With my tape recorder now in place and set to "Pause," I sat and waited for the moment the testimony would begin, when I would press "Play" and record whatever history was left.

I was once again surprised by all manner of developments. I heard these top officials of the former government denying that they knew that black people were being routinely murdered by its agents—denying even that words such as "eliminate" and "neutralize," "wipe out" and "destroy" meant to kill, despite the fact that the people whose names appeared as the direct object of those verbs had indeed ended up dead.

At some point, Archbishop Tutu, outstanding in his scarlet cassock and cap, moved to intervene. "In our experience as black people," he said, "it was happening all over. If you got into trouble with police, you were going to get clobbered and we took that as a natural part of what was happening in this country. . . . It was not the policy of the state security council, it was not the policy of the cabinet, but it was happening and the question we are trying to find an answer for is: How does an aberration become such a universal phenomenon. . . . Who is the mastermind behind this thing?"

At the end of the day, the room and everything in it had been transformed in my mind. It was no longer ordinary, and I no longer felt that I had missed out on the historic moment. Indeed, it was ongoing, as I was to learn in countless other hearings I would attend over the rest of the life of the commission. I would hear time and again that "ultimate sound," hear that "ultimate denial," hear that "ultimate moral authority"—the unassailable rightness of a position, as often expressed by "the Arch," as Desmond Tutu was affectionately known. I would hear, too, the voices of those who would denounce these proceedings as being fairer to the perpetrators—the murderers and torturers, many of who received amnesty even when their "truth" was found wanting— than to the victims, most of who have yet to receive compensation beyond their opportunity to tell their stories and unburden their souls. I would not hear, no one would ever hear, from the architects of apartheid an answer to the question, "Who is the mastermind behind this thing?" The truth commission process is now almost over, but there are many South Africans whose sense of justice has not been assuaged or satisfied. What will satisfy them? Who knows? One woman in Sebokeng, whose husband left home one day and never returned, told me that all she wanted were the bones of her husband, and that she would not rest until she got them.

The other day, as I was preparing to go to work, now as the Johannesburg bureau chief for CNN, I was listening, as usual, to an early morning talk show. As usual, the people on the show were engaged in an intense debate—South Africans love to debate—this one about the role of the state in ensuring an education based on morality. The participants on the program had strong opinions and were encouraged to express them. The deputy minister of education, a Catholic priest who came to his present role via the liberation struggle, was the lightning rod for the debate. The people calling in were black and white, and individuals from both racial groups attacked as well as defended the minister's position. Sometimes these debates can become quite esoteric, as this one did from time to time. But, for the most part, it was a stimulating exchange among people clearly struggling to define what kind of society they want and what kind of democracy they hope their new system will turn out to be. It was a long way from the debates still churning over justice, truth, and reconciliation. But it struck me that this was what the Truth and Reconciliation Commission was ultimately about. The commission had helped to create the space for words and not weapons. The space for the tender roots of a new democracy to take hold. The space for those still seeking justice to continue their pursuit without fear.

To understand this singular achievement and its effect on South Africa's transformation from apartheid to democracy, which many have called "a miracle," students of the process like Dorothy Shea, a seasoned observer of world events, are invaluable. For she has taken us beyond the "rough draft" of history that we journalists produce and given us a kind of classic study that will endure.

Charlayne Hunter-Gault
Johannesburg, September 2000

PREFACE

My first assignment as a foreign service officer was in South Africa. Living in Johannesburg from 1992 to 1994, I witnessed some of the most exciting historical events of my lifetime. Although these were still difficult times in South Africa—with senseless violence a constant menace—promise was in the air. That promise culminated in May 1994 with the inauguration of Nelson Mandela as the first democratically elected president of that country. I remember being intrigued by talk of a Truth and Reconciliation Commission (TRC), planning for which was already under way when I returned to Washington, D.C. Little did I know that I would have the opportunity to return to South Africa and study the TRC in depth.

In carrying out this study, I have been mindful of the impressive and growing body of literature on transitional justice and I have tried to avoid duplicating the important work that has already been done. I have also been keenly aware that much about South Africa is sui generis—few societies have endured anything akin to the systematic repression and the myriad indignities that occurred each day under apartheid. It is largely for these reasons that I have focused on the political context in which the TRC process has been played out, looking for lessons that might be pertinent to other societies contemplating establishing truth commissions. No truth commission can be completely insulated from politics; the stakes are too high.

I am extremely grateful to the Council on Foreign Relations for awarding me the International Affairs Fellowship that allowed me to conduct this study. I also wish to thank the United States Institute of

Peace—in particular, Joe Klaits, who directs the Jennings Randolph Fellows program, and Neil Kritz, who leads the Rule of Law program—which warmly welcomed me as a guest scholar. I am thankful, too, to John Stremlau and the University of the Witwatersrand's International Relations Department for the opportunity to serve as a guest lecturer.

I am indebted to many colleagues and former colleagues at the Department of State, especially my former boss, Greg Craig, in addition to Alan Romberg and Steve Morrison, and other colleagues on the Policy Planning Staff: thanks for believing in my ability to see this project through and for all the times I bounced ideas off you and they came back better than I ever could have formulated them. Many colleagues outside of government were likewise helpful in providing leads and encouragement; in particular, I would like to thank Ambassador Donald McHenry and Pauline Baker. Many friends and colleagues indulged me by listening to my endless monologues about the TRC. Some were even kind enough to read early drafts of the manuscript.

I was fortunate to have the opportunity to meet with and interview many of the leading experts in the field of transitional justice; I am grateful for their generosity in sharing their time and imparting their expertise. Finally, I owe a debt of gratitude to scores of South Africans: commissioners and staff of the TRC; politicians, journalists, and opinion leaders who took the time to meet with me; and, most importantly, the "ordinary" South Africans who shared their stories with me.

I continue to be inspired by the vision and sacrifices that made the TRC what it was: more than an institution, it was a process of, by, and for the South African people. It is too early to evaluate the TRC's long-term success or failure, just as it is impossible to predict how, in concrete terms, South African society will change as a result of this process. But it is not unreasonable to look for indicators of the politics at play, as well as their implications, and this is what I have attempted to do.

I concluded most of my work on the manuscript for this book in August 1999, after which I returned full time to the State Department, where I have been privileged to work for David Scheffer, the ambassador-at-large for War Crimes Issues, and where I have tried to apply some of the lessons I learned in the course of this study. I look forward to continuing to do so in my new position at the National Security Council. Having completed this study in August 1999, I regret that I have not been able to update this book except in respect of those areas that have seen significant developments. But I am pleased to report that, as the TRC's amnesty process continues to run its course, my findings remain the same.

The views represented in these pages are mine alone; they do not necessarily reflect views of the National Security Council or the U.S. State Department, which generously allowed me to undertake this study.

The South African Truth Commission

Human beings suffer,
They torture one another,
They get hurt and get hard.
No poem or play or song
Can fully right a wrong
Inflicted and endured.

The innocent in gaols
Beat on their bars together.
A hunger-striker's father
Stands in the graveyard dumb.
The police widow in veils
Faints at the funeral home.

History says, *Don't hope*
On this side of the grave.
But then, once in a lifetime
The longed-for tidal wave
Of justice can rise up.
And hope and history rhyme.

So hope for a great sea-change
On the far side of revenge.
Believe that a further shore
Is reachable from here.
Believe in miracles
And cures and healing wells.

Call miracle self-healing;
The utter, self-revealing
Double-take of feeling.
If there's fire on the mountain
Or lightning and storm
And a god speaks from the sky

That means someone is hearing
The outcry and the birth-cry
Of new life at its term.

—Seamus Heaney
from *The Cure at Troy*

1

INTRODUCTION

I accept the report as it is, with all its imperfections, as an aid that the TRC has given to us to help reconcile and build our nation." So said President Nelson Mandela of South Africa at the October 29, 1998, ceremony at which Archbishop Desmond Tutu, chairperson of the South African Truth and Reconciliation Commission (TRC), handed over the commission's Final Report.[1] Mandela went on to observe that

> the wounds of the period of repression and resistance are too deep to have been healed by the TRC alone, however well it has encouraged us along that path. Consequently, the report that today becomes the property of our nation should be a call to all of us to celebrate and to strengthen what we have done as a nation as we leave our terrible past behind us forever.

With characteristic grace and style, Mandela set the tone for a ceremony that was mired in controversy and could have been a disaster—for the TRC as well as for his party, the African National Congress (ANC). While Mandela took the moral high road in accepting and publicly releasing a report that the ANC had launched an eleventh-hour court interdict to block, his heir apparent, then deputy president Thabo Mbeki, along with several other senior ANC officeholders, did not bother to make an appearance at the ceremony.[2] The ANC was not alone in its indignation, nor were its leaders alone in boycotting the ceremony. Naysayers from the right—from the National Party (NP) to the Inkatha Freedom Party (IFP) to the Freedom Front (FF)—all found fodder in the Final Report for public denunciation.[3] For its part, the Democratic Party (DP) was content to focus its admonitions on the reactions of its political opponents, rather than on the TRC itself.[4]

Meanwhile, Tutu, ever the proselytizer of truth and reconciliation, intoned, "Let the waters of healing flow from Pretoria today as they flowed from the altar in Ezekiel's vision, to cleanse our land, its people, and to bring unity and reconciliation." And so the spectacle of the handover of the TRC's Final Report epitomized in many ways the politics that characterized the TRC process as a whole.

How, one might ask, did such a noble exercise degenerate into such naked political maneuvering? This dénouement was a far cry from the dignified solemnity that characterized the human rights violations hearings, at which victims testified about the abuses they had endured. The commissioners had wisely decided to launch the TRC process in April 1996 with these hearings to set a victim-centered tone for the commission's work. Held in civic centers, town halls, and churches across the country, these hearings always featured a lighted candle to memorialize South Africa's victims of political violence. Opened with prayers and accompanied by hymn singing, the human rights violations hearings represented the commission's—and the country's—attempt to restore honor and dignity to the victims and survivors, by giving them a platform from which to tell their highly emotive stories. In the process, South African audiences heard firsthand from victims of torture, rape, and abductions, and they heard from widows, widowers, and surviving family members about the loss of their loved ones.

Stories like that of Joyce Mthimkulu, who testified at one such hearing, have become part of the national consciousness in South Africa. Ms. Mthimkulu testified about her son, Siphiwe Mthimkulu, a political activist in the Eastern Cape who was detained on a number of occasions, tortured, poisoned with thallium (which resulted in the loss of hair and confinement to a wheelchair), and ultimately disappeared. Ms. Mthimkulu bemoaned the fact that she had never been able to give her son a proper burial (this became a common refrain in victims' hearings) and she showed the commission all that she had left of him—a clump of hair that had fallen out as a result of his poisoning.

Stories like this remind one of what the TRC process was all about. Although nothing can undo the harm that was done, these stories underscore the importance of ensuring that such abuses never recur. This book is written with the victims of South Africa's political violence in mind—recognizing that deliberation on the subject of the TRC will amount to little if it is not informed by the sacrifices made by such victims and society's debt to them.

Much has already been written about truth commissions in comparative perspective, and about the TRC in particular.[5] This study assumes some familiarity on both counts. Truth commissions, it seems, are in vogue. Priscilla Hayner, an independent researcher and noted scholar of truth commissions, has identified twenty-odd variations of this kind of mechanism in the past twenty-four years.[6] Of those, some are more noteworthy than others. The South African commission is one of the best-conceived, best-funded, and well-staffed mechanisms of its kind, and the media attention it has received is unrivaled. It is also the most ambitious truth commission to date, with a mandate that includes taking measures to restore dignity to victims and granting amnesty to eligible perpetrators of gross human rights violations, in addition to establishing as complete a picture as possible of the nature, causes, and extent of gross human rights violations that took place inside and outside of South Africa's borders between 1960 and 1994.[7] The TRC's relative success or failure, therefore, offers significant indicators of the extent to which truth commissions will persist as a tool for future transitioning societies trying to come to grips with past abuses.

This position is based on the assumption that if truth commissions collectively are perceived to be little more than feel-good exercises—if they fail to produce concrete results in terms of establishing as complete an account as possible about past abuses, restoring dignity to those who were victims of those abuses, and charting a credible course for moving beyond those abuses as a society—then those assuming power in transitioning societies will be less willing to countenance such mechanisms, regardless of how strenuously those who were responsible for atrocities under the former dispensation might lobby for them.[8] By the same token, Western donors who are asked to underwrite future truth commissions will consider the track record of previous commissions and, in the event of disappointing results, will be less inclined to fund similar endeavors in the future. Given the unprecedented media attention the TRC has received, it will likely serve as an important point of reference for both transitioning societies and Western donors.

Beyond questions about support and funding for future truth commissions looms the prospect of external meddling. Extradition and trials in foreign countries may await those who benefit from domestic amnesties, as demonstrated by the recent case of former Chilean dictator General Augusto Pinochet, whose extradition to Spain on counts of torture was recently considered by the English courts.[9] Similarly, although the Rome Treaty, which established the new International Criminal Court (ICC), does not explicitly address recognition of domestic amnesty programs, most observers anticipate that the court will, at a minimum, preserve its prerogative to intervene in cases where international humanitarian law has been violated with seeming impunity.[10]

There is no clear road map as to how judgments such as these ultimately will be made. Hayner has noted the need for international standards for credible, effective truth commissions.[11] Such standards, if and when they are agreed on, could not only serve to guide architects of future truth commissions but also serve as benchmarks for *post facto* quality assessments. They could also help the ICC navigate the murky waters of amnesties and truth commissions. In the meantime, this study draws from and expands on Hayner's proposed guidelines to assess the South African TRC process. While it is still several generations too early to judge the TRC's ultimate success or failure, it would be irresponsible not to step back and look at the TRC's broader implications. In so doing, it should be emphasized that the conclusions drawn are, by necessity, of a preliminary nature.

For all the flaws in the TRC process, it is no great stretch to credit the TRC—even at this early stage—with providing a remedy to the persistent ignorance and denial in South Africa about apartheid-era atrocities. Many commentators have pointed out that, after two years of a daily barrage of media stories generated by TRC hearings, it is no longer possible for the average South African credibly to deny the nature and extent of the gross human rights violations that took place under the old regime and during the country's transition to democracy. This in itself is a remarkable achievement, and it is one that should be kept in mind as the TRC process is subjected to critical scrutiny in the following pages and elsewhere.

In that vein, this study seeks to contribute to the existing scholarship by examining some of the key innovations in the South African model, whose architects benefited from lessons learned in other countries with similar mechanisms. It also considers a variety of ways in which the South African political backdrop informed the TRC process, and vice versa. The commission was established as an independent body that would operate free from external political interference—whether from the government, political parties, or other influential actors. But it was born of political compromise and, by the very nature of its mandate, it remained to the end, like any truth commission worth its salt, an inherently political body. The high-stakes politics of the handover of the TRC's Final Report clearly illustrate this reality.

On the assumption that truth commissions will outlast the fad stage, this book draws lessons from the South African experiment with truth telling and accountability. It is worth conceding up front, however, that the TRC's ultimate success or failure will depend greatly on two key factors beyond its control. The first concerns the extent to which the TRC's recommendations are acted upon by the government and by the institutions that fostered a climate conducive to the systematic and gross abuse of human rights under apartheid. The outcome will largely be a function of the political will of the government, which will play both implementing and enforcing roles vis-à-vis the TRC's recommendations. These roles will entail a difficult resource-allocation balancing act between urgent claims for basic quality-of-life improvements for South Africa's previously disadvantaged majority (for instance, water, low-cost housing, job creation) and many of the longer-term objectives embodied in the report's recommendations (for example, human rights training). How individual reparations for victims of gross human rights violations will fit into this equation remains to be seen.

A second factor is more nebulous but no less important. It concerns the fact that the long-term prospects of success ultimately will rely on individual South Africans—because it is on the individual level that reconciliation takes place and the seeds for societal transformation are planted. As the Final Report states, "Only if the emerging truth unleashes a social dynamic that includes redressing the suffering of victims will [the TRC] meet the ideal of restorative justice."[12] Here, political leadership, as Mandela has so aptly demonstrated, can play an immensely powerful role.

2

THE BENEFITS OF LEARNING FROM OTHERS' MISTAKES

Timothy Garton Ash has identified three main paths—trials, purges, and history lessons—by which countries have come to terms with human rights abuses by their former governments. "The choice of path, and the extent to which each can be followed," he writes, "depends on the character of the preceding dictatorship, the manner of the transition, and the particular situation of the succeeding democracy."[1] Among many other advantages, those in South Africa who planned, negotiated, and worked on the TRC had the benefit of being in a position to learn from the experiences of several other countries that had enacted amnesties, truth commissions, and other mechanisms to deal with their past. As negotiations in South Africa progressed—from secret talks between Nelson Mandela and President P. W. Botha, to the unbanning of the ANC, the return and indemnification of exiles, and the release of political prisoners, to "talks about talks" and the multiparty negotiations leading to the Interim Constitution —politically motivated violence and human rights abuses continued to plague South Africa. Therefore, the relevance of ensuring a process of accountability for such acts became increasingly apparent.[2]

Ash cites Tina Rosenberg's distinction that "in Latin America, repression was deep, in Central Europe it was broad" as helpful in explaining the different paths chosen in those respective regions.[3] South Africans contemplating their own path might reasonably have questioned how South Africa fit into this paradigm, as repression in apartheid South Africa was both deep ("there was a group of people who were clearly victims—tortured, murdered, or . . . 'disappeared'") *and* broad (it was the majority black population that suffered the most and "was kept down by millions of tiny Lilliputian threads of everyday mendacity, conformity, and compromise").[4] Furthermore, beyond the repressive tactics the apartheid state exercised against the majority nonwhite population, South Africa's political landscape was complicated by widespread intercommunal violence, ostensibly between the predominantly Zulu IFP supporters and their ANC rivals. Finding that more people died in the unprecedented levels of violence during 1990–94 than during the preceding thirty years (the TRC's mandate ran from 1960 to 1994), the Final Report confirmed the widely held view that such violence was orchestrated and stoked by a "third force"—agents of the apartheid state and security forces who sought to derail progress toward democratic rule by demonstrating that South Africa would be "ungovernable" under black rule.[5]

Although a number of countries had successfully made a transition from authoritarian rule to democracy, no country had endured a system akin to apartheid, which the international community had singled out in its opprobrium, labeling it a crime against humanity. So negotiators would return, time and again, to the particularities of the South African context. Kader Asmal, who was then minister for water affairs and who played an influential role in the early thinking about the TRC, reflected at the time:

> there is no prototype that can be automatically used in South Africa. We will be guided, to a greater or lesser extent, by experiences elsewhere, notably in those countries that managed to handle this highly sensitive—even dangerous—process with success. But at the end of the day, what is most important is the nature of our particular political settlement and how best we can consolidate the transition in South Africa.[6]

In the view of Graeme Simpson, executive director of the Centre for the Study of Violence and Reconciliation (CSVR), Latin American examples were primarily instructive as "examples of failure rather than success," and it was with a view "to redressing the errors made in these countries, as well as to acknowledging the differences in the unique South African context," that nongovernmental organizations (NGOs) such as the CSVR submitted recommendations on the TRC legislation.[7]

Long before most South Africans became cognizant of such issues, NGOs such as the Institute for Democracy in South Africa (IDASA), Justice in Transition, and the CSVR were establishing contacts with practitioners and intellectuals from other countries with experience or expertise in truth commissions or similar mechanisms.[8] Under the leadership of Alex Boraine, who would later be appointed as deputy chairperson of the TRC, Justice in Transition sought insights and lessons learned from prior truth commissions and facilitated brainstorming, networking, and lobbying efforts for some thirty South African NGOs.[9] According to Boraine, a healthy consultative dynamic developed, largely because "those in the human rights community welcomed the opportunity to do something *for* rather than something *against*—something *for* the future."[10] Based on this extensive "homework," South African civil society was instrumental not only in shaping the public debate about the need for some kind of accountability mechanism but ultimately in crafting the TRC legislation: Boraine and company were responsible for the first working draft of the legislation.[11]

The ANC had the benefit of its own experience, having appointed the Skweyiya and Motsuenyane Commissions in 1991 and 1993, respectively, to investigate allegations of torture, killings, and other abuses at ANC detention camps. In response to the Motsuenyane Commission's recommendation that it do so, the ANC's National Executive Committee publicly apologized to its victims, assuming collective responsibility for the human rights abuses that occurred.[12] But the ANC was also anxious to put in proper perspective the abuses committed by its members, given that the vast majority of human rights violations in the South African context were committed by agents of the apartheid state. Following up the concept first mooted in Kader Asmal's inaugural lecture as professor of human rights law at the University of the Western Cape, the ANC called publicly for a truth commission, "similar to bodies established in a number of countries in recent years to deal with the past," to investigate *all* human rights violations, including those committed by the apartheid state and its agents.[13]

The NP, meanwhile, had counted on being able to indemnify the apartheid security forces from prosecution in the new dispensation and indeed fought for a blanket amnesty until the last moment. The issue was a deal breaker for the NP. The ANC was sensitive to the danger in "pushing the other side into a corner where the only option out is to fight" and felt the need to "preempt what was a very real possibility of a right-wing insurrection."[14] And so the ANC agreed to the NP's demand that there be some kind of amnesty. Objecting in principle to self-amnesty, however, the ANC was savvy enough to save for a later day the battle to balance its amnesty concession with provisions that would help meet the needs of those who had suffered under apartheid.[15] In a late-night negotiating session, after the main body of the Interim Constitution had been agreed on, the parties agreed to include a post-amble, whose formulation left it to a democratically elected parliament to work out the precise mechanism under which an amnesty regime would be implemented.[16]

After over three hundred hours of parliamentary debate, the National Unity and Reconciliation Act emerged, a product of consultation, debate, compromise, and determination. The Truth and Reconciliation Commission that it created was deliberately made different from any truth commission that had preceded it. It is worthwhile to reflect on some key examples of how lessons learned in other parts of the world were reflected in the innovations in this TRC.[17] Specifically, this study will address the TRC's unique power to grant amnesty on an individualized basis; its robust powers of search, seizure, and subpoena; and its contextualized approach to sketching the truth about the past. It is useful to keep in mind the constraints and advantages South Africa faced in putting the TRC's powers into practice, as well as the extent to which the intended outcomes had practical effect.

PROBLEMS WITH BLANKET AMNESTY

Consider, for example, the lesson on blanket amnesty that Jose Zalaquett, who served on the Chilean National Commission for Truth and Reconciliation, shared with his South African interlocutors at one of the pre-TRC consultative conferences referred to above:

> One should begin by reconciling oneself to the idea that amnesties are possible. However, several things should first take place:
>
> ▸ amnesty should possibly serve the ultimate purposes of reparation and prevention;
>
> ▸ it should be based on the truth, or one cannot really know what the pardon or amnesty is for;
>
> ▸ there should ideally be an acknowledgement of that truth; and

▶ the amnesty must be approved democratically in the sense that it must be the will of the nation to forgive.[18]

Zalaquett's advice struck a chord with those in the audience who would become the architects of the TRC. The compelling need to establish the truth—and for an acknowledgment of that truth—was seen as particularly important for victims. Out of such concerns was born the most significant innovation associated with the TRC: there would be no blanket amnesty offered to all perpetrators of gross human rights violations under the ancien regime and during the transition; instead, individuals would have to apply for amnesty for their politically motivated acts, omissions, or offenses, and that amnesty would be conditional, among other things, on full disclosure. The Final Report explains this key innovation:

> No other state had combined this quasi-judicial power with the investigative tasks of a truth-seeking body. More typically, where amnesty was introduced to protect perpetrators from being prosecuted for the crimes of the past, the provision was broad and unconditional, with no requirement for individual application or confession of particular crimes. The South African format had the advantage that it elicited detailed accounts from perpetrators and institutions, unlike commissions elsewhere which have received very little cooperation from those responsible for past abuses.[19]

Harvard law professor Martha Minow has succinctly captured the logic of this innovation: the legislation "turns the promise of amnesty, wrested from political necessity, into a mechanism for advancing the truth-finding process."[20] Furthermore, for those not already in the dock, the carrot of amnesty is coupled with the stick of possible prosecution for those who either do not come forward to apply for amnesty or are unsuccessful in doing so, according to one or more of the conditions set forth in the act.[21] Willie Hofmeyr, an ANC member of Parliament and one of the key negotiators of the act, has explained that the requirement for individual rather than group amnesty applications was intended in part to "undermine the solidarity of the security forces," who otherwise presumably would conspire to conceal the truth.[22] A certain degree of uncertainty among perpetrators about who had come forward and what they had said could help provide a stronger incentive for perpetrators to apply for amnesty. It was hoped that because the deadline for amnesty applications came well before amnesty hearings had been concluded, this uncertainty would be heightened, as would the act's ambiguity about the admissibility of information that emerges out of amnesty hearings in subsequent prosecutions.[23] Lyn Graybill has opined that the act "disallows court use of confessions given before the Amnesty Committee as evidence," but notes that "confessions may nevertheless alert attorneys general to the culprits in unsolved cases, and they may then prosecute them on the strength of their own investigations."[24] In fact, it remains to be seen how broadly the act's limitations will be interpreted by the courts. Meanwhile, as late as June 1999, the Amnesty Committee had not developed a clear policy on which information could and should be shared with the National Director of Public Prosecutions (NDPP), beyond the point of departure that "an amnesty application cannot be used as an affidavit in a court of law."[25]

In reality, the threat of prosecution as incentive for perpetrators of gross human rights violations to come forward had mixed results. For starters, the threat of civil suits was never particularly credible. First, most South African victims cannot afford the costly legal expenses associated with bringing a civil suit.[26] Second, there is a three-year proscription (statute of limitations) for most civil claims in South Africa. In addition, claimants must be able to prove intent, which is difficult in the best of circumstances. In most cases, the facts, including the perpetrators' identities, were not known. As long as the perpetrators kept their silence, it would stay that way.

Where there was credible threat of prosecution, results were more favorable. The criminal trial of Eugene de Kock, the notorious South African Police (SAP) hit-squad commander, demonstrated the potential deterrent value of a robust prosecutorial strategy. In August 1995, Kock was convicted of eighty-nine charges, ranging from murder to fraud, and was sentenced to two life terms plus 212 years.[27] Believing that he had been betrayed by the political leaders of the apartheid state in whose name and under whose authority he professed to have carried out these crimes, de Kock implicated several ranking SAP officers and former cabinet officials.[28] Many of those implicated subsequently applied for amnesty.

A similar dynamic, it was hoped, would develop in the amnesty process. In some cases, it did. For example, several midlevel police officers who applied for amnesty for firing indiscriminately into a crowd of protesters in 1992 implicated then head of the Security Police, General Johan van der Merwe, as the one who gave the order. Van der Merwe in turn applied for amnesty for his involvement in several incidents, and in the process of disclosing relevant information, he implicated two cabinet-level officials. One of those officials, former minister of law and order Adriaan Vlok, went on to implicate former president P. W. Botha in the 1988 bombing of the headquarters of the South African Council of Churches (SACC).

Meanwhile, however, in 1995 the KwaZulu-Natal attorney general, Tim McNally, botched the prosecution of former defense minister Magnus Malan and sixteen other top officers of the former South African Defense Force (SADF) who had been charged with organizing hit-squad activity that resulted in the murder of thirteen people in KwaMakutha in 1987. As Ash points out, in the aftermath of the Malan trial, the threat of prosecution lost credibility, and "without that stick, the carrot of amnesty is useless."[29] It comes as no surprise, then, that the amnesty-for-truth exercise yielded more fruit from among the ranks of the former SAP, where the de Kock trial had effectively broken the code of silence—and the threat of prosecution was more credible—than it did with the former SADF, whose solidarity was reinforced by Malan's acquittal.

The logical conclusion of a conditional amnesty is that, if the conditions for amnesty are not met, prosecution is possible, if not probable. It therefore came as something of a surprise when, in the aftermath of the handover of the Final Report, the issue of a general amnesty once again raised its head. Journalist Max du Preez pointed out the irony in hearing "the very same arguments that I heard three years ago against the establishment of a truth commission" used by ANC members in support of a post-TRC blanket amnesty: "Let's forget the past . . . this will only divide our nation; it will be bad for reconciliation; it will lead to violence."[30] The political motivations and implications of this development are discussed in greater detail later in this book. In the meantime, it is worth pondering the extent to which South Africa really did benefit from the Latin American "lesson" on the ill effects of a blanket amnesty, given the notion's resurrection. What are the implications for future truth commissions? The short answer is that all amnesties are imperfect, even conditional amnesties, and the politically expedient pull of blanket amnesties should never be underestimated.

THE NEED FOR ROBUST INVESTIGATORY POWERS

South Africa was not the first country to encounter difficulty in enticing former members of abusive security forces to break ranks to tell the truth about past abuses. Commenting about the obstacles faced by the Chilean truth commission, Zalaquett noted that "while witnesses and possible perpetrators were invited to testify," they could not be forced to do so; "subpoena powers would have been an effective tool."[31] Simpson echoed this concern, noting that the considerable limitations on the Chilean commission's investigative powers meant in practice that it was unable "to effectively elicit the necessary information about the 'disappeared' . . . [or] attribute individual responsibility for past human rights abuses."[32]

Given that the National Party's political leadership and top military brass had long operated according to the principle of "plausible deniability" and that, as former TRC executive secretary Paul Van Zyl has pointed out, many of the political crimes to be investigated were "committed by highly skilled operatives trained in the art of concealing their crimes and destroying evidence," it became clear that the TRC, if it was going to have any success in fulfilling its mandate, was going to need ample investigative muscle.[33] And so the drafters introduced the innovation of a permanent Investigation Unit and provided for a number of specific investigative powers, including the powers of subpoena, search, and seizure.

Under Section 29 of the act, for example, the TRC could subpoena a person to appear before it and answer questions relevant to a particular investigation. Thematic hearings of this nature included inquiries into the Vlakplaas (hit squad) operations; violence perpetrated by the Civil Cooperation Bureau (CCB); the role of security police in KwaZulu and Natal; the Mandela United Football Club; and the apartheid state's chemical and biological warfare program. As further remedy, Section 32 of the act lays out robust search-and-seizure powers. Anticipating problems associated with the widely reported destruction of sensitive documents by the previous government, the TRC's mandate also includes the requirement to "determine what articles have been destroyed by any person in order to conceal violations of human rights or acts associated with political objectives."[34]

In practice, the TRC had difficulty exercising its enhanced investigatory muscle. The Investigation Unit was hampered both by a lack of policy direction in the early phase and by delayed receipt of funding. The fact that "public hearings were launched in mid-April 1996, before the Investigation Unit was fully established and prior to the formulation of any policy regarding the selection of matters for public hearings," is testament to this reality.[35] That there would be a political imperative to move expeditiously in holding human rights violations hearings is understandable. But this impulse, however well intentioned, was shortsighted. Piers Pigou, a former investigator with the unit, has said that "not nearly enough has been done to uncover the past," in part because the Investigation Unit was "plagued by organizational, managerial, and bureaucratic problems."[36]

Subsequent reorganizations allowed the Investigation Unit to assume a more proactive role, though difficulties remained and it encountered a great deal of resistance, in particular in attempting to access information from the government. The commission had agreed, somewhat naively, to the use of "nodal" (liaison) points through which all requests for information and responses were channeled between the Investigation Unit and both the South African Police Service (SAPS) and the South African National Defense Force (SANDF), which merged the former apartheid-era SAP and SADF with personnel serving in structures parallel to the former liberation movements. But instead of facilitating access to relevant information, appointed officials in those agencies often played more of a censoring role. Such obstructionism is not surprising, given that the majority of the bureaucrats who staffed those agencies had worked under and presumably had loyalties to the old regime.[37]

Former TRC research staffer John Daniel decried the obstructionism that characterized the SANDF's manipulation of the nodal-point system:

> Throughout the life of the Truth Commission, the SANDF did this [obscene gesture] to the commission. . . . For more than a year, the SANDF successfully blocked access of the Research Department to the military archives. Meeting after meeting with the result of promise after promise led to nothing. We received no help at all from the fact that the minister of defense and his deputy were ANC members. They were either unable or unwilling to clear a path through these doors. It was not until April of 1998, a mere six months before the report was due out, that access was given, and it was given on a highly constrained basis. We were

allowed to request files . . . but we were told that they did not exist, that
they were destroyed, or "we can't find them." We had no way of check-
ing whether that information was true. We were refused access to an index of the holdings. Even those files that were shown to us were first
sanitized by a legal team attached to the SANDF.[38]

Daniel's point about the unwillingness or inability of the ANC ministers to intervene to facilitate the TRC's access to information in
SANDF archives is worth remembering in future scenarios: one cannot assume that support from the political leadership will translate into
operational support from functionaries, particularly those who were
affiliated with the old order. TRC commissioner Dumisa Ntsebeza, the
head of the Investigation Unit, has said that in retrospect he regrets that
the TRC did not use its search-and-seizure powers more effectively:
"Consciously or unconsciously, we imposed our own constraints. We
did not want to upset the apple cart, and we wanted to give those
within the regime a chance."[39]

Of course, a much more aggressive use of search, seizure, and subpoena powers with the security forces might have backfired, resulting
in even less information being made available to the TRC, and it probably would have necessitated costly legal battles. It is this reality that
prompted Fazel Randera to comment, "I still have divided feelings on
whether, if we had been much more robust, we would have gotten
much more information."[40] At a minimum, however, the early flexing
of the TRC's enhanced investigative muscle could have sent a strong
signal to individual perpetrators and could have brought significant
pressure to bear on those who were sitting on the fence. Lamenting
this missed opportunity, Simpson said, "It's about showing your teeth
early in the process."[41] The commission's failure to adopt a more
robust approach in exercising its powers of search, seizure, and subpoena early on is linked to the perception on the part of many perpetrators that the threat of prosecution lacked credibility, and this
perception emboldened the alleged perpetrators to adopt an arrogant
and defiant posture toward the TRC and the amnesty process. This
attitude was not confined to the security forces. In 1996, IFP leader
Mangosuthu Buthelezi publicly announced that the IFP would not
cooperate with the TRC, and IFP members were discouraged from
applying for amnesty.[42] Only two NP cabinet officials applied for

amnesty; P. W. Botha and F. W. de Klerk conspicuously refrained. Botha even went so far as to defy the commission's subpoena.[43] This flouting of the TRC's authority has left significant gaps in the commission's truth recovery effort and left South Africa with a large pool of unrepentant perpetrators facing possible prosecution, a political hot potato if ever there was one.

THE BENEFITS OF A CONTEXTUAL APPROACH

In the chairperson's foreword to the Final Report, Archbishop Tutu honored the victims who came forward for their public testimony about the abuses they suffered: "They were generous in their readiness to make themselves vulnerable; to risk opening wounds that were perhaps in the process of healing, by sharing the often traumatic experiences of themselves or their loved ones."[44] There is no denying the profound impact on South Africans of the highly emotive human rights violations hearings that the TRC held around the country had. But for each of the 21,300 victims who came forward to make a statement, there were plenty who did not. So, even coupled with the amnesty process, which also held public hearings at which perpetrators were legally bound to disclose their criminal acts, substantial parts of the truth about the past were not revealed.

It is in this context that one can best appreciate Zalaquett's counsel that South Africa's truth commission would need to "balance between case by case . . . and contextual references."[45] The act incorporated this advice by mandating that the TRC reckon with the complexities that characterized and influenced political violence in South Africa. The TRC was to make findings on "the nature, causes and extent of gross violations of human rights, including the antecedents, circumstances, factors, context, motives, and perspectives which led to such violation."[46] The TRC's interpretation of this part of the mandate led to another important innovation in the continuum of truth commissions: the holding of thematic and institutional hearings. Van Zyl discussed the logic in this: "We felt that it was impossible to paint as complete a picture as possible unless we looked at the institutional and systemic dimensions," and that the TRC could not meet the act's requirement to recommend administrative, institutional, and legislative measures designed to prevent future human rights abuses "unless we understood the institutional causes of them."[47]

Specifically, the TRC held event hearings, or "window cases," at which victims, alleged perpetrators, and experts participated, so as to explore thoroughly the context of a specific event, deliberately selected because it was considered representative of broader patterns of abuse. Special hearings on children and youth and on women complemented this effort by looking at patterns of abuse experienced by those specific groups. Finally, the TRC also held institutional hearings, "exploring how various social institutions contributed to the conflicts of the past."[48] These hearings played a positive role by shedding light on and provoking public debate about the roles that many institutions had played as silent partners of apartheid. Specifically, the TRC invited representatives from the health sector, the judiciary, the media, the business sector, faith communities, and the prison system to testify; as these hearings went on to show, institutions such as churches, hospitals, the judiciary, and private businesses had to varying degrees acquiesced to—and benefited from—the apartheid system.

Some of the institutional hearings were more successful than others, however. Circumstances permitting, these hearings offered the added potential benefit of serving as catalysts to institutional change from within. Van Zyl points out, for example, that the TRC's hearings on the health sector prompted an internal process within the organized medical profession to review its code of ethics.[49] But circumstances were not always permitting. Participation in some of the institutional hearings, for example, was quite disappointing. Most judges and magistrates, citing concerns that participation would somehow compromise their independence, declined to attend the institutional hearing on the judiciary; only a few sent in written responses. The Final Report addresses their nonparticipation with disdain:

> The failure of the judiciary to appear is all the more to be lamented when the historic significance of the Commission is considered, as well as its envisaged role in the transformation of South African society into a caring, humane and just one. The Commission was thus denied the opportunity to engage in debate with judges as to how the administration of justice could adapt to fulfil the tasks demanded of it in the new legal system; not so as to dictate or bind them in the future, but so as to underline the need

urgently to re-evaluate the nature of the judiciary. . . . The Commission deplores and regrets the almost complete failure of the magistracy to respond to the Commission's invitation, the more so considering the previous lack of formal independence of magistrates and their dismal record as servants of the apartheid state in the past. They and the country lost an opportunity to examine their role in the transition from oppression to democracy.[50]

Beyond the missed opportunities referred to above, the judges' and magistrates' nonparticipation suggests that concrete steps to follow through in transforming the judiciary will be taken grudgingly, at best. The same holds for those business representatives who halfheartedly participated in the institutional hearing on business and labor, taking the position that, because they did not actively or deliberately plan or participate in human rights violations, they were effectively exempt from making submissions. Their stated purpose in participating in the commission was, rather, "to promote understanding of the role of business under apartheid and to explore areas where business failed to press for change."[51] This is a far cry from the ANC's position that "historically privileged business as a whole must . . . accept a degree of co-responsibility for its role in sustaining the apartheid system of discrimination and oppression over many years."[52] The passive-voice recommendations that came out of this hearing reflect the difficulty the TRC encountered in reconciling contrasting perspectives on institutional responsibility, as well as the difficult road that lies ahead.[53]

Nonetheless, these thematic and institutional hearings collectively did help the TRC to avoid the pitfall of looking at specific cases of human rights abuse in isolation. They also allowed the TRC to highlight the institutional and societal legacies of apartheid, such as the vast and egregious disparity that still exists between rich and poor. Finally, the thematic approach permitted the TRC to get away from a strict victim-perpetrator approach to address the role of beneficiaries of apartheid as well.[54] That both individuals and institutions who benefited from apartheid showed some reluctance to acknowledge as much comes as no surprise and can be ascribed, in part, to the common mentality among whites that "I won't pay because I'm not guilty, I was not one of the perpetrators."[55] The prevalence of this mentality, which is reflected in a March 1996 public opinion poll of white South Africans, does not bode well for voluntary compliance with suggested reparative measures such as a wealth tax.[56] Again, political leadership will be key to achieving greater acceptance on the part of apartheid's beneficiaries of the notion that they have some degree of responsibility in this regard.

3

THE POLITICS OF THE TRC

Many onlookers would have liked for the TRC to be above politics. But it would have been foolhardy to expect an institution that was born of political compromise, that has operated in a politically charged environment, and whose mandate includes such politically loaded concepts as truth, reconciliation, and amnesty to be anything but political. Michael Sharf has observed that truth commissions are

> inherently vulnerable to politically-imposed limitations and manipulation; their structure, mandate, resources, access to information, willingness or ability to take on sensitive cases—even the wording of the final report—are all largely determined by political forces at play when they are created.[1]

Although Sharf may overstate the argument, one can certainly make this case with respect to the TRC, and it provides a useful point of departure for this discussion about the politics of the TRC. In fact, it may also be useful to take Sharf's analysis a step further: One can also anticipate that the political forces to which he referred will evolve over time, that they will continue to influence public debate about the commission, if not the commission itself, and that the proceedings of the commission, depending on their scope and visibility, may also play a role in altering the political landscape.[2] This is not to suggest that the integrity of the TRC was compromised, that it did the political bidding of any party or leader, or that it will be solely responsible for making or breaking any political careers. But there should be no illusion: the TRC process was a profoundly political undertaking.

Not surprisingly, the TRC was routinely accused of political bias, most vociferously by the IFP and NP, but also by the ANC and other parties. To the extent that these accusations were made across the political spectrum, one could argue that the TRC came out of the process with increased credibility. Unfortunately, however, any such credibility carried a high political cost. The ANC's frustrations with the commission were completely lost on the IFP, which criticized the TRC, its commissioners, and staff throughout the process, and which essentially refused to cooperate with the TRC.[3]

Much about the TRC process is unique to South Africa, because of the particularities entailed in addressing its apartheid past. But all truth commissions take place in a political context. It is therefore worthwhile to consider a number of illustrative examples of how politics influenced the TRC process—and vice versa. This brief examination of the politics of the TRC is not confined to the question of who applied political pressure and why, although that is certainly important; it looks as well at questions of appearances, "spin," and political consequences. TRC commissioners and staff were well aware of the political ramifications of their actions and decisions, and they contemplated and debated such matters. In fact, they were often on guard against political pressure and indeed went out of their way to avoid even the perception that the TRC was subject to outside influence. Such evasive actions do not make it any less a political body; rather, they are evidence of the kinds of political forces at play. The point is not to criticize the TRC or, for that matter, those parties that may have attempted to influence it or use it as a political tool, but rather to better understand the dynamics of such politicization. From a prescriptive point of view, one might turn the logic of Sharf's observation around to consider how the political reality that provides the backdrop to a truth commission can be a strength, rather than a weakness, in the pursuit of truth and reconciliation.

THE SELECTION OF COMMISSIONERS

The selection of commissioners proved to be a highly visible political exercise, the effects of which would influence virtually every aspect of the TRC's work. Aside from serving the largely symbolic function of leading the commission and setting the tone for the overall process, those who would be selected as commissioners would be tasked with directing the work of the TRC's three committees (on human rights violations, reparations and rehabilitation, and amnesty) as well as the Investigation Unit. Furthermore, though much of the drafting of the Final Report—most notably, the findings and recommendations—would be left to TRC staff, the commissioners would have the final say over the report's substance. The stakes were thus quite high.

The act stipulates that "the Commission shall consist of not fewer than 11 and not more than 17 commissioners," and that "the President shall appoint the commissioners in consultation with the Cabinet."[4] The act also specifies that the commissioners must "not have a high political profile."[5] It is interesting to note that the act left open the possibility of the appointment of up to two non–South African commissioners. Several truth commissions that preceded the TRC had incorporated varying degrees of foreign participation; international involvement in the leadership is often indispensable in conferring legitimacy on a truth commission's work. It is not surprising that this route was not taken in the South African context, however, due to persistent political sensitivities about outside influence.[6]

Mandela opened up the selection process for even wider public participation than was called for in the act by inviting nominations from the public. A selection panel composed of members of civil society and government considered these nominations and narrowed down a list of some three hundred to a short list of twenty-five, from which Mandela, in consultation with his cabinet and, significantly, the heads of the political parties, selected fifteen. Two additional appointments not from the short list—Khoza Mgojo and Denzil Potgieter—were added to make a total of seventeen commissioners, apparently to render the commission more representative.[7] Mandela later revealed that he had not personally approved of all of his appointees, but that he had appointed them, in spite of his reservations, in the interest of national unity.[8]

Although the commissioners' racial and gender composition was not strictly proportional to that of society at large, the selection process clearly reflected a deliberate political attempt to achieve a high degree of representivity. The result was a commission composed of seven women and ten men; the racial breakdown was seven blacks, six whites, and two each of "coloured" and Indian extraction. The commissioners also spanned the political spectrum in their affiliations. Despite the good intentions that brought it about, this very representivity, which yielded starkly contradictory views about human rights violations in South Africa's past, let alone the political and moral accountability for such, was a recipe for inertia when it came to interpreting the mandate and making tough political decisions. To be fair, though, part of the problem can probably be attributed to the large number of commissioners at the helm. Van Zyl has commented that the diverse composition of the TRC's policymaking organ left Tutu and Boraine with the never-ending task of trying to minimize the contradictions; eliminating them was out of the question.[9] Boraine noted the practical effect: "Commissioners had a great deal of difficulty finding each other and working with each other, which meant we spent a lot of energy on maintenance, rather than on getting the job done."[10] Racial undertones—and outright racism—further complicated the dynamics. As Boraine said, "there was a great deal of racism within the commission itself. People were very quick to judge and to undermine."[11] The Final Report refers to these challenges only elliptically, but clearly they were at the core of many of the commission's problems.[12]

THE POLITICS OF THE AMNESTY PROCESS

The issue of how the amnesty process would be administered was contested from the start, and the Amnesty Committee's decisions have frequently been second-guessed. Part of the initial controversy stemmed from one of the compromises the NP had successfully lobbied for in the Government of National Unity (GNU) cabinet: that amnesty hearings would be held behind closed doors. The provision was unacceptable to human rights groups, especially coming on the heels of the revelations that, on the eve of 1994 elections, President de Klerk, without consulting the ANC, had allowed some three thousand people, including high-ranking police, military officers, and cabinet officials, to be secretly indemnified.[13] Human rights NGOs and media organizations mounted a successful campaign to amend the legislation, with the result that amnesty hearings involving gross violations of human rights would take place in public, except where doing so would defeat the ends of justice.[14] The act laid out objective criteria for the granting of amnesty:

▶ the application must comply with the requirements of the act;

▶ the act, omission, or offense to which the application relates must be an act associated with a political objective; and

▶ the applicant must make full disclosure of all relevant facts.[15]

In addition, the original draft of the legislation put forward by Justice in Transition would have had one of the commissioners serve as secretary of the Amnesty Committee. The Amnesty Committee would have made recommendations on granting or denying amnesty; the commissioners would have taken final decisions. Another option contemplated would have had recommendations on amnesty vetted by the president. The NP objected to these proposals, arguing that the Amnesty Committee, composed of judges, should be independent from the commission itself. The NP's aim was to insulate the quasi-judicial decision making on amnesty from political influence and potential bias. Ultimately, the NP was successful in its bid to establish an Amnesty Committee as part of the commission itself, but with independent decision-making authority. Indeed, there are sound reasons for an autonomous Amnesty Committee—any suggestion of bias could sully the whole process—but the provision also had unforeseen consequences. As Boraine lamented in retrospect, "something of the spirit of the commission was not transferred to the Amnesty Committee."[16]

An anecdote about the committee's early amnesty decisions illustrates the practical impact of Boraine's observation. In the early batches of decisions handed down by the Amnesty Committee, a pattern seemed to establish itself whereby white applicants were refused amnesty, whereas black applicants were successful. To put the potential impact of this trend in context, one need only consider the wariness with which white perpetrators approached the amnesty process. Of this, Lyn Graybill wrote that, "initially, perpetrators were slow to come forward as many were waiting to see how judges interpreted such ambiguous clauses of the amnesty legislation as 'politically-motivated acts' and 'proportionality to objectives.'"[17] At one point in the process, when a commissioner learned that the Amnesty Committee was on the verge of publicly releasing another batch of amnesty decisions that would have continued this troubling pattern and perpetuated the perception that whites were routinely being refused amesty, the commissioner intervened. An exchange between the commissioner and an Amnesty Committee representative was said to have gone something like this: "Are there not *any* successful white applicants?" "Oh yes, but they're not quite finalized." "Well finalize them *now*! Don't you realize that these decisions have consequences!"[18] That the Amnesty Committee was apparently oblivious to the political signals it was sending when it announced those early decisions—whether or not as a result of its strictly quasi-judicial function—points to one of the downsides of its complete independence.

And then there is the Amnesty Committee's decision to grant amnesty to the thirty-seven ANC leaders (including Thabo Mbeki) who had applied for amnesty, not for any specific act, but based on the notion of their collective responsibility for any human rights violations perpetrated by ANC members in the course of the struggle against apartheid. Misunderstandings abound with respect to these applications, the Amnesty Committee's initial decision to grant amnesty, the subsequent court challenges, and later reversal. Political parties (and their leaders) seized on those misunderstandings to further their respective political objectives. Charles Villa-Vicencio, the former director of research for the TRC, summed it up well: "It was a bad application that was handled badly by the TRC, and was made even worse by the response of the deputy president."[19]

That there were no specific details about actual violations of human rights in the amnesty applications of the ANC leaders is not necessarily as insidious as some of the opposition parties have suggested. The ANC has maintained that those ANC leaders who applied for amnesty in this group had not personally been involved in executing or ordering any actions that would constitute gross human rights violations; rather, the applications were a symbolic gesture. The positive take on the applications of the "ANC 37" is that the ANC was sending a political signal to its rank and file to the effect, "We leaders accept ultimate responsibility for the excesses committed by comrades in furtherance of what was a just cause—the struggle against apartheid; you too should cooperate with and participate in the TRC process." In addition, the ANC was trying to set an example for the other political parties' leaders, particularly former presidents de Klerk and Botha and the former leadership of the police and defense forces. The intended message to them was more of a challenge: "We accept political and moral responsibility for excesses committed by our comrades; will you do the same on behalf of your security forces?"

The chairperson of the Amnesty Committee, Justice Mall, presided over the panel that initially granted amnesty to the group. Van Zyl downplayed the role of political pressure in this case but suggested that the fact that the ANC was the ruling party may have "subliminally influenced their decision."[20] However commendable the ANC's gesture may have been, the Amnesty Committee's decision to grant amnesty was not in keeping with the act's requirement of full disclosure; the applications disclosed nothing. Furthermore, the fact that the decision came without any public hearings stoked public perceptions that the ANC had cut itself a deal with the TRC. That scores of midranking ANC members and former soldiers of Umkhonto we Sizwe (Spear of the Nation, the military arm of the ANC, popularly known as MK) also submitted applications accepting responsibility for the armed struggle but completely lacking in details about the acts for which they sought amnesty further undermined the credibility of the ANC's claim to the moral high ground. Presumably, midlevel cadres would be privy to at least some operational details about which political leaders could legitimately have claimed ignorance.

The commissioners, meanwhile, were baffled by the Amnesty Committee's lack of political—let alone judicial—judgment. The atmosphere within the TRC in the aftermath of the announcement was one of panic; the commission's credibility was on the line. Boraine was said to be furious, Tutu appalled.[21] Fazel Randera commented: "To this day, I still cannot understand how leading judges and advocates could have sat, looked at the act, what their mandate was, and given these people amnesty."[22] The TRC barely beat the NP to the punch in taking its own Amnesty Committee to court, but the decision to do so was not uncontested. Ntsebeza, for example, has maintained that those ANC leaders who applied for amnesty did so only because of their "association with the liberation movement under whose name human rights violations occurred. . . . It was a legitimate application."[23]

By taking its own Amnesty Committee to court, the TRC was indirectly taking on the ANC. Van Zyl opined that "if an illustration were needed of impartiality, this would be it."[24] Unfortunately, however, the damage had already been done to the Amnesty Committee's credibility, and it is not clear that the public understood the distinction between the TRC's Amnesty Committee and the TRC proper. And so any positive aspects of both the symbolic gesture on the part of the ANC and the resoluteness on the part of the TRC were overtaken by the high-decibel partisan reactions and accompanying media frenzy that greeted the Amnesty Committee's initial decision.

It should be noted that this was not the first time the TRC had taken on the ANC: earlier in the process, Tutu had threatened to resign in the face of statements from ANC leaders to the effect that, because the ANC had fought a "just war" against the apartheid state, ANC cadres need not apply for amnesty.[25] Ultimately, the ANC and the TRC were able to resolve the immediate problem—with the result that the ANC officially encouraged its members to apply for amnesty and Tutu agreed to stay on as chairperson—but the underlying issue of the ANC's perceptions of inappropriate evenhandedness in the context of the "just war" would come back with a vengeance. The subpoena issued to Winnie Madikizela-Mandela, the ANC Women's League (ANCWL) president and the former wife of Nelson Mandela, in connection with the killings and beatings in the late 1980s of Stompei Seipei and others represents another high-profile incident in which the TRC took on the ANC, or at least one element of it.[26]

The NP brought its own court application to have the amnesties of the ANC 37 declared illegal, an action that served its purpose of discrediting both the ANC and the TRC. Meanwhile, the ANC was left in the unenviable position of trying to defend the bona fides of its gesture when the terms and the tone of debate had already been set—much to the ANC's disadvantage.[27] The media was complicit, focusing more on the hyperbole of the debate than on the complexities of the case.

In March 1999, the Amnesty Committee handed down a decision reversing itself and rejecting amnesty: "In so far as the applicants seek to apply for amnesty for acts committed by their members on the basis of collective political and moral responsibility, their applications fall outside the ambit of the . . . Act and accordingly they do not require to apply for amnesty."[28] Predictably, opposition parties took the opportunity to score political points. The New National Party (NNP, the successor party to the "old" NP), for example, suggested that the ANC leaders would now be liable for criminal and civil prosecution and that "all this is of their own doing because the ANC leaders were less than truthful . . . and played games with the TRC when they lodged their amnesty applications."[29] For its part, the IFP directed its criticism at the TRC itself: "The legal challenge to the TRC concerning 'the ANC 37' has revealed a staggering example of confusion, incompetence or something even more sinister."[30] Sinister forces, it seems, make good political fodder. On a campaign stop in Gugulethu township outside Cape Town, Winnie Madikizela-Mandela suggested that sinister forces were responsible for the timing of the TRC's refusal to grant amnesty to the ANC leaders just before the election.[31]

This is not the only amnesty decision subjected to close scrutiny or used for political gain. Take the decision to refuse amnesty to Janus Walusz and Clive Derby-Lewis, who were convicted of the April 1993 murder of Chris Hani, the leader of the South African Communist Party. When the Amnesty Committee denied amnesty on grounds that the applicants failed to fully disclose the details of their actions and found that they lacked political motivation as required in the act, several predominantly white Afrikaner opposition parties promptly denounced the decision and accused the Amnesty Committee of giving in to political pressure.[32] Similarly, when the police officers involved in the 1977 killing of Black Consciousness activist Steve Biko were refused amnesty, the *Citizen* editorialized about the bias it perceived in the amnesty decisions, noting that the "Amnesty Committee says the killing of Mr. Biko was 'not an act associated with a political objective.' Extraordinary. How much more political can you get?"[33] Other amnesty decisions in high-profile cases have drawn similar criticism, but the record shows that, on balance, the Amnesty Committee's decisions did not reflect any bias in favor of one party over any other.[34]

Those who served on the Amnesty Committee did encounter some pressure from political parties, but in the words of one, it was "an indirect pressure," and its aim was not to influence individual amnesty decisions but to prompt the committee to finish its work as quickly as possible.[35] To this end, party leaders conveyed the message by letting the committee know that "funds will not be available forever" and through public statements to the effect that, "We would not want to let the work of the Amnesty Committee interfere with the election."[36]

One final aspect of the amnesty process that deserves attention is the decision to extend the amnesty cutoff date from December 6, 1993 (the date the negotiations for an Interim Constitution and multiparty democracy concluded), to May 10, 1994 (when President Mandela was inaugurated). The Final Report explains the decision, which required an amendment to the Interim Constitution:

> The extension of the cut-off date for amnesty applications . . . was a reminder of the transitional context in which this unique, accountable amnesty process needed to be understood. The extension of the date was due largely to pressure by, on the one hand, the white right-wing (the Afrikaner Weerstandsbeweging [AWB] and Afrikaner Volksfront) which opposed the elections by violent means and, on the other, black groups such as the Pan Africanist Congress (PAC) and Azanian Peoples Liberation Army (APLA), which had continued the "armed struggle" during the negotiation process. It became clear to the commission in the course of its work that such an extension would enhance the prospects of national unity and reconciliation, because it would allow these groupings to participate in the amnesty process.[37]

That the TRC itself lobbied Parliament to extend the cutoff date marked a significant shift in the politics of the TRC. Graeme Simpson has criticized the TRC's decision to actively lobby as "a most fundamental political compromise [that] demonstrated a willingness to play politics on the part of the TRC. Prior to that, the TRC could claim that, whatever they were doing, they were doing no more than administering in some senses a compromising political agreement reached by the ANC and the National Party in the negotiation process."[38] Others have defended the lobbying, pointing out that it was done in the face of the ANC's opposition to the idea of an extension. The rationale, according to Van Zyl, was that the election was a more natural cutoff date; groups such as the PAC and AWB, who had at best a marginal influence in the multiparty talks—the conclusion of which marked the act's original cutoff date—had stopped engaging in violence after the election; to insist on the original, more arbitrary, date, he said, "smacked of selective justice."[39] Both arguments have merit, but on balance it seems that the TRC should have erred on the side of caution, refrained from active lobbying, and let others make the sound argument in favor of the later cutoff date. Furthermore, if, as many have conjectured, the TRC lobbied for extending the cutoff date in order to foster greater goodwill on the part of the right-wing groups, one should note that that effort was not particularly successful.

THE POLITICS OF REPARATIONS (OR NOT)

The act charges the TRC with making recommendations with respect to granting reparations to victims, including urgent interim measures, but reserves the power to implement those recommendations—that is, allocating and appropriating the requisite financing for reparations payments—for the president in consultation with Parliament. Only when the president's proposals are approved by Parliament is the government empowered to make the necessary regulations.[40] This requirement marks a departure from the act as originally drafted, which would have allowed the TRC to determine compensation on its own. That the politicians would so insert themselves in the process is understandable, given the fact that large sums of money would be involved. But the fact that the legislation left the commission without the ability to implement its own recommended reparations policy has had profound consequences. In the words of the Final Report, "reparation is essential to counterbalance amnesty," but the commission's mandate left it with a "glaring" contradiction between its ability to deliver amnesty and its inability to deliver reparations.[41] This lack of symmetry has been exacerbated by delays. With regard to the urgent interim measures, the Amnesty Committee's formulation of a recommended policy took longer than expected, and there were further delays in the government's promulgation of regulations to deliver them. The first such payments (starting at a baseline of R2,000, approximately $333) were not made until July 1998. Similarly, the government's failure to move forward on the individual reparations grants as recommended in the Final Report has contributed to the perception on the part of many victims that they have been shortchanged.[42]

The Final Report explains the rationale for its recommended individual reparations grants:

> The individual reparation grant is an acknowledgement of a person's suffering due to his/her experience of a gross human rights violation. It is based on the fact that survivors of human rights violations have a right to reparation and rehabilitation. The individual reparation grant provides resources to victims in an effort to restore their dignity. It will be accompanied by information and advice in order to allow the recipient to make the best possible use of these resources.[43]

The maximum individual reparation grant would total R23,023 ($3,837) per annum for a six-year period and would be administered by the President's Fund. The exact amount would vary, according to a formula that would differentiate between rural- and urban-dwelling victims (based on the assumption that health services are 30 percent more expensive in rural areas) and factor in the number of dependents and/or relatives (up to a maximum of nine). The projected budget is R477,400,000 ($79,566,666) per annum, adding up to a six- year total of R2,864,400,000 ($477,400,000).[44] With stakes this high, it is not surprising that the country's political leaders would want to scrutinize the policy and subject it to a thorough cost-benefit analysis.

What is of concern, however, are the increasing signals that the ANC is leaning toward not granting individual reparations at all. Consider some public statements regarding reparations: In February 1999, the ANC's secretary-general, Kgalema Motlanthe, suggested that the government was more inclined to make reparations to communities than to individuals.[45] Soon thereafter, presidential spokesman Parks Mankahlana confirmed that this was the substance of the government's recommendation, but that the cabinet had yet to take a decision. Mankahlana justified the government's position thus: "How do you compensate a person who left school because of police harassment? . . . When we reduce this into rands and cents then we are not addressing the whole notion of reconciliation."[46] Mbeki's parliamentary statement on the TRC's Final Report sent mixed signals on this question. He indicated that "we must also attend to the matter of individual reparations, both in the form of cash and the provision of services," but he also said that government should not insult the dignity of victims by trying to compensate them with money. He hinted that the ANC's preference was for community-based reparations that would benefit all victims of apartheid, saying that all South Africans must be "ready and willing to provide reparations to entire communities, by helping to pull them out of the wretched conditions which are the product of a gross and sustained violation of their rights as human beings."[47]

This policy has come as a surprise to those TRC commissioners and staff who had worked on the recommended reparations package, in consultation with relevant government ministers. Charles Villa-Vicencio recalled numerous meetings with government ministers at which the individual reparations grants proposal was hammered out. "In fact," he said, "certain ministers agreed that that was the correct approach."[48] An

ANC politician disagreed, opining that it was unfortunate that the Reparations Committee declined to take on the delicate problem of how to differentiate between compensation packages according to the circumstances of individual victims: "I don't know who they got the nod from, but I don't think they got it from the top. And I suppose that whoever gave them the nod was also afraid to bite the bullet. They had been given resources to make individualized proposals and they just . . . came up with a blanket formula."[49]

But one can easily understand why the Reparations Committee chose to finesse the delicate problem of trying to put a monetary value on suffering. Van Zyl spoke eloquently about the TRC's deliberations on this vexing issue:

> How can you differentiate between someone who was psychologically tortured, physically tortured, lost a loved one, lost a breadwinner, or a two-year-old child? Do you do means testing? Is it worse to lose a hand or a foot? Or to be blind or paralyzed? Every one of our instincts was to differentiate, because it seems to be an absurdity that someone who was in detention for one day and was slapped around and received electric shocks once should receive the same reparations as someone whose entire family was killed. It just doesn't seem right. It doesn't seem commensurate. But as soon as you start to differentiate, there are all these anomalies; you can't differentiate in a coherent way. And so we would keep on going back to the commission with all these criteria, like need, severity, impact, etcetera. After eighteen months, the commission decided that there was tremendous wisdom in equality because this is, after all, a symbolic payment.[50]

Beyond the question of individualization, the ANC considered the recommended reparations package to be "an absolutely disastrous proposal," because the TRC "went way outside what is a fairly clear conception of the law, that financial reparations would be a fairly token thing."[51] The ANC's concern is apparently that the seemingly generous grant recommended by the TRC risks creating two classes of victims, those who were victims of gross human rights violations and those who were merely victims of the everyday indignities and hardships under apartheid. As a matter of policy, the ANC would not want to compensate one class of victims at the expense of the other, especially when those other victims are also still facing hardships associated with the legacy of apartheid. As Van Zyl has pointed out:

Successor regimes inevitably face a multitude of demands from constituencies who expect their quality of life to improve under democracy.
Reparations paid to victims of gross violations of human rights represent a
diversion of resources from developmental spending on housing, education or health care—all areas that would benefit a broader section of society. This prioritization of a specific category of victims over a more general
group of disadvantaged citizens is more difficult to defend when the policies of the prior regime resulted in both poverty and human rights abuse.[52]

It is conceivable that the ANC's sensitivity on this issue stems from
memories of the provision of financial assistance to returning exiles in the
early 1990s, which led to division between the ANC members who had
been in exile and stood to benefit, and those who had stayed in the country and did not. It would follow that the ANC would not want to
reawaken or exacerbate those tensions by providing reparations grants to
victims of gross human rights violations at the expense of the other victims of apartheid, who may have suffered just as much, if not more.
Ironically, the TRC's recommended reparations package was modeled to
some extent on the previous grants made available to MK soldiers returning from exile.[53]

Simpson has criticized this position: "I sympathize with the
dilemma, but it's a marvelous excuse for doing nothing."[54] Those
responsible for the recommended reparations policy are none too pleased,
either. As early as April 1998, Hlengiwe Mkhize, the chairperson of the
Reparation and Rehabilitation Committee, was cautioning about the need
for a clear signal from the government about its commitment to individual reparations grants; more recently, she has said she believes there is still
a chance for individual reparations grants, in spite of all the signals to the
contrary from the ANC.[55] Commissioner Yasmin Sooka has also spoken
out against the government's apparent disregard for victims.[56] Naturally,
the ANC's approach does not sit well with the victim community, many
of whom have come to expect individual compensation, in spite of bold-
faced disclaimers such as those that appear in the TRC's pamphlet on
reparations: "Please remember that these are proposals to the President.
The President and Parliament will make a final decision on them."[57]

What is not yet clear is whether such discontent on the part of victims
will develop into a more serious political liability for the ANC. It was surprising that the nondelivery of reparations was not a widely debated

issue in the 1999 election campaign. Two factors may help explain why this was the case: first, it was hard to compete with the hot-button issues that defined the campaign, such as crime, corruption, and the delivery of housing, electricity, water, education, and jobs; second, the victim community lacked sufficient political clout to register on the national political radar screen. As victims groups become better organized, these dynamics could well change, especially as the "Mandela factor," which has kept the majority of the population loyal to the ANC, fades.[58]

THE POLITICS OF THE ENDGAME

Nobody anticipated the whirlwind of legal challenges and political maneuvering that would usher in the release of the Final Report. The high drama that accompanied the public release of the report soured the overall political atmosphere and provoked bitter reactions. Lines were drawn and prospects for reconciliation looked dim, as political parties, commissioners, and commentators traded scathing sound bites. That the truth and reconciliation process would be reduced to such spectacle is unfortunate. In retrospect, however, it is useful to consider the politics that were at play, because they highlight the high stakes of the TRC process as a whole.

The impetus for much of the ensuing drama was the TRC's transmittal of Section 30 notifications, which gave advance notice to those against whom the TRC intended to make derogatory "findings" in the Final Report. The TRC so notified former president de Klerk, whom it was to declare "an accessory to gross human rights violations," because, among other things, in failing to report that he had known about unlawful acts committed by the state's security forces (for example, the 1988 bombing of the SACC headquarters), he had "contributed to creating a culture of impunity within which gross human rights violations were committed."[59] Contesting the legitimacy of the findings, de Klerk launched an urgent court interdict to prohibit the TRC from publishing them. He and the TRC reached a settlement in which the TRC agreed temporarily to expunge from the Final Report derogatory findings about him.[60] De Klerk's last-minute settlement was conspicuously evidenced in the equivalent of one page of text that was dramatically blacked out in the Final Report. Somewhat ironically, in light of the ANC's own legal challenge that would soon follow, then justice minister Dullah Omar challenged the logic behind de Klerk's interdict and defended the TRC's prerogatives: "The Commission must be allowed to boldly, courageously and without interference speak its mind in the report."[61]

In the Section 30 notification it sent out to the ANC, the TRC indicated that it planned to find the ANC morally and politically responsible for gross human rights violations, including the indiscriminate killing of civilians by ANC land mines and bomb attacks, in addition to the torture, severe ill treatment, and execution of alleged spies. The ANC was incensed at the perceived "criminalization" by the TRC of the liberation struggle and at the "moral equivalence" and "artificial evenhandedness" with which the TRC treated abuses by the liberation movements, on the one hand, and those by the former government and security forces, on the other hand. An indignant ANC leaked the offending findings and demanded a meeting with TRC commissioners. The ANC wanted to make the case that it had waged a "just war" against apartheid, which was recognized as a crime against humanity. Therefore, it would argue, abuses committed by those in the ANC should be seen as "inseparable from the consequences of legitimate struggle."[62] Critically, however, in focusing its energies on a face-to-face meeting, at which it intended to make this case, the ANC failed to respond in writing to the TRC within the designated fifteen-day deadline.

The commissioners were deadlocked over how to respond to the ANC's request for a meeting. Tutu, who was in the United States at the time, was called on to cast the deciding vote. He voted against meeting with the ANC leadership on the grounds that it would entail bending the regulations for the ruling party, which would be both inappropriate and unfair.[63] Those who voted with him were also troubled that such a meeting would create the appearance of the TRC succumbing to political pressure from the ANC, a concern the ANC described as "utter rubbish."[64] The evidence would suggest, however, that the ANC was not above trying to exert political pressure on individual commissioners. One commissioner with ties to the ANC spoke frankly on the subject: "There were several conversations I had with different people who were saying, 'Look. Protect yourself. There's life after the Commission. . . .' These were fairly senior people, including someone who was very senior in the government who was saying that to me. And sure, that did actually increase the pressure."[65] Another commissioner commented, "Yes, there was political pressure. And it got ugly. I wouldn't have thought that this would come from comrades. . . . Such is the arrogance of power."[66] Press leaks on both sides fueled the increasingly explosive political climate.

With the face-to-face meeting route effectively closed, the ANC turned to a different tactic. Apparently taking its cue from de Klerk, the ruling party launched a late-night court interdict the night before the handover ceremony was scheduled to take place. The interdict sought to prevent the TRC from publishing its Final Report unless and until it had taken into consideration the ANC's response to the derogatory findings against it. On the morning of October 29, 1998, the case was dismissed with costs, allowing the handover ceremony to go forward.

Suggesting that the ANC action smacked of abuse of power, Tutu had vowed to fight the ANC's interdict "with every fibre in my being," adding, "I have struggled against tyranny. I did not do that in order to substitute another tyranny."[67] Tutu's characterization of the ANC as a new "tyranny" reportedly angered some of his fellow commissioners, and the following day Tutu publicly apologized for "my self-righteousness, my arrogance."[68] If these developments stirred division within the TRC, the effect was equally inflammatory within the ranks of the ANC. In the aftermath of the failed attempt to block publication, several ANC politicians voiced their embarrassment and displeasure, though most did so anonymously, saying, for example, that the court application was "absolute nonsense . . . God only knows where that decision was taken and how it was taken" and that the move was "unbelievably stupid."[69] Several ANC cabinet ministers, members of the National Executive Committee, and premiers also reportedly expressed their personal regrets to Tutu and other commissioners.[70]

It became clear in the subsequent days and weeks that Mbeki, as ANC president, was behind the decision to launch the court interdict; Mandela, it was said, had been consulted, but he did not have a say in the decision. The strong insinuation was that, although he objected to the offending findings, Mandela disagreed with the strategy of pursuing a legal challenge, and his posture at the handover ceremony would seem to confirm that. To the extent that there was a split within the

ANC on the question, it seems to have been along the following fault line: those who had fought to keep the armed struggle within the parameters of international norms and standards—and this was primarily the ANC leadership who had been in exile—were said to be most bitter about the findings, which offered little in the way of acknowledgment of their efforts, and, in their view, "criminalized" the disciplined and just war the ANC had fought against apartheid. ANC leaders who had remained in the country had less of a personal stake in this issue and thus were more sanguine about the findings.[71] The media played up the significance of this apparent split in the ANC, inferring troubling indicators about Mbeki's "authoritarian" leadership style.[72]

In light of the ensuing political fallout, it is worth revisiting the ANC's (over-)reaction to the substance of the Final Report. First, the ANC's leadership should not have been caught off guard, because, as many have pointed out, there were no surprises in the Final Report. The TRC's findings on the ANC, in fact, were based primarily on information that the ANC had provided in its submissions to the TRC. As one ANC MP commented, "There was nothing new in what the commission found . . . it wasn't new until we made it news."[73] Beyond that, one should consider the troubling implications of the poisoned atmosphere that characterized the endgame. The widespread disdain for the TRC within the ruling party does not bode well for early or enthusiastic implementation of the TRC's recommendations, particularly those that are politically sensitive or financially costly, such as reparations.

THE POLITICS OF PROSECUTIONS (OR NOT)

The Final Report recommends that, "where amnesty has not been sought or has been denied, prosecution should be considered where evidence exists that an individual has committed a gross human rights violation . . ."[74] In the aftermath of the release of the Final Report, the recently appointed NDPP was repeatedly asked whom among those implicated in the TRC process he would prosecute, and there has been a great deal of speculation in the South African media on the question. Bulelani Ngcuka indicated obliquely that, in the interest of national reconciliation, some cases should not be prosecuted.[75] The implicit logic is that certain prosecutions would provoke political violence, which would be contrary to the goals of national reconciliation. Cases where prosecutions would provoke violence and political instability, it follows, should not be pursued. Renascent violence in the highly volatile province of KwaZulu-Natal illustrates the point; one need only imagine the widespread political violence that would ensue, for example, were the NDPP to prosecute IFP leader Mangosuthu Buthelezi or other prominent IFP leaders. Both the underlying assumptions and the logic of this argument are certainly open to challenge, however. CSVR senior researcher Hugo van der Merwe took them on in an editorial in the *Sunday Independent:* "It would be a grave mistake to equate political stability with genuine reconciliation. It may have been necessary to grant amnesty for the sake of the transition to democracy, but we cannot justify the extension in response to veiled threats of violence from implicated political leaders."[76] Similarly, the *Star* editorialized:

> If we are now going to accept the spurious argument that peace and reconciliation depend on a blanket amnesty for the warmongers of KwaZulu-Natal, and the torturers and murderers of the innocent, who had an opportunity to come clean, that would be a kick in the teeth for those who believed in the integrity of the process. And it would lend credence to the suspicion that vote-catching next year is everything to the political parties leading the crusade for blanket amnesty, and the country be damned.[77]

Many observers were surprised that talk of a general amnesty—in whatever guise—which had been dismissed in the context of the multiparty talks leading to South Africa's transition, resurfaced in late 1998. The scramble to come up with a politically acceptable post-TRC amnesty provision would seem to suggest that the ruling party failed to think through what would happen to those high-profile alleged perpetrators against which the TRC would make derogatory findings. Perhaps the ANC leadership and other architects of the TRC just wrongly assumed that those very perpetrators would have applied for and received amnesty. Hofmeyr disputed this interpretation, arguing that the drafters of the legislation were fully aware of the possibility that security forces would boycott the amnesty process. At any rate, the ANC is not united on the question of general amnesty; those who lost loved ones—particularly to the orchestrated political violence between the ANC and IFP that swept KwaZulu-Natal and the East Rand in the early 1990s—may not be so quick to forgive their former adversaries, particularly those who shunned the amnesty process, as most IFP supporters did. Some commentators have even suggested that such a move could provoke a split within the ranks of the ANC.[78]

Although Mandela spoke out strongly against general amnesty, pledging to resist it "with every power I have," the ANC has continued to flirt with the idea.[79] Whatever the mechanism, de facto or de jure, whether by extending amnesty deadlines, by creating a new amnesty regime exclusively available to those who were party to political violence in KwaZulu-Natal, or by exercising political control over which cases the NDPP chooses to prosecute, there are clear indications that the ANC is actively considering the available options for avoiding prosecutions. Indeed, as recently as May 1999, Mbeki suggested in an interview that a mechanism for collective amnesty should be introduced to accommodate apartheid-era generals, among other groups; Omar later confirmed that Mbeki had asked him "to draft legislation that would allow groups of former soldiers and freedom fighters and members of political parties to apply for amnesty without specifying individual acts of human rights violations."[80] A skeptical *Business Day* editorial posed difficult questions about the proposed scheme: "What of the thousands of individuals who approached the commission in the belief that if they failed to get amnesty, they faced prosecution? And how does the idea of an indiscriminate pardon square with the government's professed commitment to rebuilding the rule of law and a human rights culture?"[81]

There have for some time been clear indications that the ANC leadership was leaning in this direction: In the parliamentary debate on the TRC Final Report, for example, although both Mandela and Mbeki stated that a general amnesty should not be entertained, Mbeki also indicated that "we will have to discuss such proposals as have been made on this matter with regard to KwaZulu-Natal and others put forward by the former generals of the SADF who have themselves confirmed their loyalty to the country and its Constitution."[82] In March 1999, Omar was reported to say that "the TRC process had bypassed the province of KwaZulu-Natal for lack of support, and there needed to be a response to the wounds caused by the human rights violations that took place there . . . there should be some process to allow the warring parties to come to terms with the past."[83]

As *Business Day* surmised, one can probably dismiss Mbeki's professed concern about enticing apartheid generals to come forward this late in the game as something of a "red herring," as there is "no evidence that they continue to pose a threat to the state"[84] Rather, the ANC's motivations appear to be twofold. First, it wants to forestall the sharp increase in political violence that many commentators have predicted would engulf KwaZulu-Natal (and possibly other parts of the country) in the event of criminal prosecution of the IFP leaders who were implicated in gross human rights violations but had shunned the amnesty process. A second but related motivation is to facilitate the rapprochement apparently under way between the ANC and the IFP. One seat shy of a two-thirds' majority in Parliament, the ANC will not need IFP votes as desperately as some had speculated it would in the run-up to the 1999 elections. But one can well imagine how the incentive of enticing IFP political support could have been a significant factor in the ANC's calculus in the run-up to the elections. In any event, IFP support will help Mbeki push his ambitious, delivery-oriented agenda through Parliament. It would not be unreasonable to assume that Buthelezi's cooperation would be contingent on the nonprosecution of any IFP leaders.

Providing for "collective" amnesties might be just the creative mechanism the ANC is seeking, so as to avoid the political fallout associated with "blanket," or "general," amnesties, while allowing it to effectively achieve the same political objective.[85] Several observers have suggested that the most likely scenario will be an extension of the existing amnesty process so as to take full advantage of the staff and structures already in place, with the legislation crafted so as not to preclude selective prosecutions of those who fall outside the ambit of the collectives covered. However, it is not at all clear that such a mechanism could withstand a constitutional challenge on the basis of the equality clause. If a collective amnesty mechanism favors some groups (that is, those who reside in KwaZulu-Natal or those who did not apply for amnesty prior to the cutoff date) over others, the Constitutional Court may well strike it down for flagrant discrimination. Mbeki will undoubtedly put the ANC's best legal minds to the task to avoid this.

In the meantime, tough choices on whom to prosecute await

Bulelani Ngcuka, the NDPP. It is not yet clear how much political influence he will be subject to in the process. For its part, the TRC has submitted to the office of the NDPP a list of one hundred alleged perpetrators for whom it recommends prosecution, and the Final Report indicated that the TRC would make available to the appropriate authorities relevant information (excluding privileged information from amnesty applications).[86] A list of names, of course, is hardly sufficient for the NDPP to open a case, and surprisingly, as of June 1999, the TRC had not yet developed a clear policy on what information in its archives it could share: "Staff from the NDPP have been here to access information . . . but there's no mechanism in place" for sharing that information, according to one Amnesty Committee staffer.[87]

Aside from what is desirable from a moral and political perspective, one must also consider the feasibility of bringing criminal prosecutions. The NDPP's choices on this matter will be influenced by practical constraints, including limited resources. Every trial of an apartheid-era perpetrator has opportunity costs in that fewer resources will be available to try ever-increasing present-day criminal caseloads. Furthermore, having been stung by the failed prosecution of former defense minister Malan and his coaccused, the state will likely pursue prosecutions only in cases that meet a high evidentiary threshold. The likely result is that no more than a handful of prosecutions will proceed from the TRC process.[88]

4

REPORT CARD

Noting the benefits and indeed appropriateness of the ad hoc nature of truth commissions, which are designed to suit country-specific conditions, Hayner has suggested that there is nonetheless a need for "minimal standards" that a truth commission should meet if it is to be considered "a serious, good faith effort and respectful of those who will be affected by its work."[1] Such standards, she has pointed out, could also "facilitate appropriate international and national oversight."[2] Hayner built on the work of Louis Joinet, special rapporteur for the UN Sub-Commission for Prevention of Discrimination and Protection of Minorities, who first proposed such guidelines in a document entitled "Set of Principles for the Protection and Promotion of Human Rights through Action to Combat Impunity."[3] The International Criminal Court, once it is operational, will doubtlessly weigh in with its own criteria for evaluating future truth commissions.[4] In the meantime, thinking on these questions will continue to evolve, and members of the international donor community, who have been called on in the past to help underwrite these mechanisms, will, based on their own assessments, vote with their checkbooks. Those people responsible for establishing truth commissions in the future could also benefit from prospective consideration of such guidelines, along with an understanding of the potential pitfalls that necessitate them. Among other things, an honest exercise of this nature could help establish whether a society is well suited for a truth commission, or vice versa. To the extent that other societies can learn from the South African experience, it would be useful to consider not only *how* South Africa measured up, but also *why*. What circumstances in South Africa lent themselves to relative success or failure in each area?

The assessment of the TRC below draws liberally from the guidelines suggested by both Hayner and Joinet to assign six benchmarks against which to evaluate the South African TRC.[5] A couple of caveats are in order. First, it would be simplistic to confine the assessment process to the TRC per se, without distinguishing among the different actors—the government, the TRC, political parties, NGOs, and others that have played a role in the process. Second, it would be a mistake to focus only on the end product; the TRC has been a process, and that process is ongoing. The relevant actors have shouldered varying degrees of responsibility at different phases of the commission's life. The categories below are grouped under philosophical/conceptual and practical/logistical categories, and they apply, as appropriate, to those who were responsible for decision making in the formative stages, those who were responsible for carrying out the TRC's mandate, and those who are responsible for implementing the TRC's recommendations. Some of the criteria require more subjective analysis than others, but it should be emphasized that the conclusions drawn at this point are only preliminary. It will take several generations before we can assess the long-term impact of the TRC. Finally, the examples cited below are illustrative and, where relevant, refer to the analysis in the preceding pages.

CONCEPTUAL BENCHMARKS

Public Ownership

Recognizing the important role that civil society can play in a truth commission process, Hayner rightly places the criterion "public participation in crafting the commission" at the top of her list, and she cites the South African model as the exception to the norm in its "extensive public participation."[6] Credit goes to a highly engaged, well-informed NGO community, veterans of similar exercises who shared their expertise with South African interlocutors, the funders who had the foresight to channel funds to support such efforts, and a responsive Ministry of Justice. Open hearings in Parliament also facilitated healthy public debate and input, evidenced most dramatically by the successful lobbying campaign to amend the legislation so that amnesty hearings would be held in public.

It was probably the human rights violations hearings that made the TRC most accessible to the average South African. TRC representatives traveled throughout the country to take statements from victims of gross human rights violations. Of the 21,300 victims who came forward, about 2,000 were invited to testify in public hearings. For many, these highly emotive hearings were the crux of what the TRC was about: those who had been victims of political violence were given a platform from which they could recount their personal histories. And it was on the basis of these stories that a common understanding of South Africa's history during this turbulent period would be built. Afrikaner poet, journalist, and author Antjie Krog captured this sentiment in celebrating the truth commission microphone "with its little red light" into which victims told their stories as "the ultimate symbol of the whole process: here the marginalized voice speaks to the public ear."[7] That this poignancy was lost on naysayers who ridiculed the TRC as a "Kleenex commission" does not detract from the important role the human rights violations hearings played, not only in helping to restore victims' dignity but also in integrating their stories into the public consciousness.

Extensive media coverage, although not without bias, was instrumental in keeping the public informed throughout the TRC process. In particular, daily South African Broadcasting Corporation (SABC) radio coverage of the TRC hearings, broadcast in South Africa's indigenous languages, made the TRC highly accessible to South Africa's rural black population. In addition, SABC television scored high viewership for its weekly *Special Report*, in which the highly regarded independent journalist Max du Preez highlighted important developments relating to the TRC.

Cumulatively, these factors contributed to a sense of public ownership, especially in the early stages. But Hayner's guidelines also explicitly provide that the lines of communication should be kept open throughout the process "to allow public feedback on the methodology and impact of the commission's work."[8] It is on this score that the TRC seems to have faltered. Having played such an instrumental role in crafting the TRC, some NGOs were shocked when the TRC, once it became operational, closed ranks. Although the TRC periodically called on NGOs to provide a variety of advisory or consultative capacities, the NGO community did not enjoy the access to or influence with the TRC that it had come to expect in the formative stages.[9] "From the point at which the commission got up and running, it became a 'fairly exclusive club,'" according to Simpson.[10]

This is not to suggest that there was not significant public feed-back—there was, through the media, through one-on-one representations by NGO representatives to individual commissioners or staff, even through public demonstrations by victims' groups. But what seemed to be lacking was the requisite responsiveness on the part of the TRC. Van der Merwe et al. attributed this difficulty of engaging effectively with the commission to several dynamics, including the inexperience of many NGOs, particularly victims' groups and peace NGOs, at lobbying, not a traditional activity for these groups.[11] Equally important, the TRC's posture vis-à-vis NGOs resulted from the internal politics of the deliberately representative commission. Those commissioners who came from politically conservative backgrounds opposed the TRC's engaging with human rights–oriented NGOs that they perceived as being too closely linked with the former liberation movements.[12] In addition, van der Merwe et al. explained the relative success of the NGO community in the lobbying phase, compared with its failure to engage in the operational phase, as a function of political dynamics. When it was politically expedient, the political parties co-opted the NGOs: "The overlaps between NGO and political agendas were effectively exploited during the lobbying phase of the TRC. However, the failure of NGOs to develop the anticipated close relationship between themselves and the TRC possibly reflects a broader tension between the competing agendas of the state and NGOs."[13]

Borrowing now from Joinet, one should also consider under this rubric the publicity given to the commission's report. Mandela, speaking of the report that "today becomes the property of our nation," did the right thing in publicly releasing the document as soon as it was turned over to him by the TRC, despite the fact that some members of his party would have had him delay release for the two months that the act would have allowed.[14] South Africa's Independent Newspapers group and the Institute for Democracy in South Africa did their part by publishing and distributing key sections of the report as newspaper supplements. When the Amnesty Committee releases its codicil to the Final Report in late 2000, the TRC will also release a 250-page "popular version" of the Final Report, which is promised to be "highly accessible" in terms of cost and readability. Finally, the TRC's outstanding Web site (www.truth.org.za) has played an invaluable role in keeping those with access to Internet technology (granted, a limited segment of the South African population) abreast of the TRC's proceedings.[15]

It is perhaps in the aftermath of the release of the Final Report that the public's involvement in the truth and reconciliation process is most critical. The hard part of the TRC process involves making choices—on individual and societal levels—accepting responsibility, and taking concrete steps to overcome the legacy of apartheid and transform society. Tutu and Boraine certainly tried to get this message across in their public comments in the run-up to the handover of the Final Report and at the ceremony itself by emphasizing that this event marked the beginning, not the end, of the process. The Final Report, too, addresses this reality: "South Africans will need to continue to work towards unity and reconciliation long after the closure of the Commission," which, in the words of a participant in one of the TRC's public meetings, "could do no more than kick start" the process.[16] As Mandela said during the parliamentary debate of the Final Report:

> Long after the Commission has folded and its offices [have] closed, political leaders and all of us in business, the trade union movement, religious bodies, professionals, and communities in general shall have to remain seized with the matters that the TRC process brought to the fore. Inasmuch as reconciliation touches on every aspect of our lives it is our nation's lifeline.[17]

Faith communities and community-based organizations are uniquely placed to perform outreach and organizing functions of this nature, but ultimately, it is on the individual level that reconciliation takes place and the seeds for societal transformation are planted.

The public's involvement in this phase will be shaped by a variety of factors. At this early stage, it will suffice to mention a few initiatives that are developing in response to the Final Report. First, aside from individual reparations grants, the TRC recommended community-based reparations, including monuments and memorials, an idea to which politicians have thus far seemed responsive. To the extent that the public can be involved in making decisions such as these, so much the better. In addition, MPs have stated their intention to have a National Summit on Reconciliation, as recommended in the Final Report. Ideally, such an exercise should be fed from the grassroots up in a transparent and inclusive process, and it should be focused on translating the TRC's recommendations into concrete programs of action to make tangible progress toward the long-term goals of reconciliation and the transformation of society.[18]

Another proposal is for a new investigative commission of inquiry that would pick up where the TRC left off. Polly Dewhirst, a researcher at the CSVR, has pointed out, for example, that despite the fact that many of the TRC's human rights violations hearings concluded with commissioners saying, "We will investigate your case," the TRC simply did not have the resources to investigate them all.[19] Such a commission could carry on investigating the many unsolved cases brought to the TRC, including the two hundred exhumation requests that were outstanding when the TRC finished its work.[20] One ANC MP indicated that he agreed in principle with the idea, but that the details would have to be thoroughly evaluated: "I think one can find some mechanism, post–Truth Commission, to help victims get more of the truth."[21] Obviously, such an ambitious undertaking would have to be thought through. The financial implications alone would be enormous. What is significant, for the purposes of this discussion about public ownership, is that proposals like this have been enunciated—that individuals and groups are seeking ways to carry on the work of the TRC.

Finally, Charles Villa-Vicencio, the former TRC director of research, is establishing an NGO called the Institute for Justice and Reconciliation in Africa that will concern itself not only with post-TRC transitional politics in South Africa but also with transitional justice issues elsewhere in the world. Some observers have questioned the credibility of this initiative, going so far as to dismiss it as "job perpetuation" for a handful of former TRC employees.[22] However, one can make a persuasive argument about the potential benefit of continuity that such an institute could provide by preserving the body of skill and expertise internal to the commission, particularly as South African society struggles to respond to the TRC's findings and recommendations. To be effective—and credible—this NGO will have to be more methodical than was the TRC in reaching out to existing networks of community-based organizations.

The Mandate

A truth commission's mandate sets the parameters for its work, defines its goals and objectives, and articulates the means through which they are to be pursued. Hayner rightly has called for TRCs to have a "flexible but strong" mandate, something for which, to the credit of the extensive public consultations referred to above, the architects of the TRC and those who provided input score high marks.[23] Charged with the following tasks, the TRC deserves credit for having the most ambitious mandate of all truth commissions to date:

▶ establishing as complete a picture as possible of the causes, nature, and extent of the gross violations of human rights during a thirty-four-year period;

▶ facilitating the granting of amnesty to persons who make full disclosure of all the relevant facts relating to acts associated with a political objective;

▶ making known the fate and whereabouts of victims and restoring their dignity by affording them the opportunity to relate their own accounts of violations that they suffered; and

▶ producing a report, including recommendations for the prevention of future human rights violations.[24]

One can debate the relative pro and cons of such an expansive mandate. One downside is that its breadth was not matched with the requisite resources for timely fulfillment, and the various objectives laid out in the act were not prioritized. In practice, the TRC recognized that it could not carry out all of the components of its mandate simultaneously, so it endeavored to set the tone for the whole process by holding victims' hearings first, along with relevant statement taking and investigations. A product of the TRC's *interpretation* of its mandate, this decision was consistent with the mandate's exemplary victim-friendly "principles to govern the Commission's dealings with victims."[25] If the restoration of victims' dignity was the TRC's top priority, this was not always apparent to victims, however.[26] To be fair, the government and Parliament are due some share of the blame on this count: delays in implementing the TRC's recommended reparations program resulted in the first "urgent interim" reparations not being delivered until July 1998, and the fate of individual reparations grants still hangs in the balance.

The commission interpreted the act's definition of "gross human rights violation" in a way that precluded ex post facto criminalization of legally sanctioned apartheid activities that violated the rights of the majority of the population, such as the mandatory carrying of pass books and the forced removal of populations.[27] Professor Mamdani, the well-respected intellectual and head of the University of Cape Town's African Studies Department, criticized the TRC for this narrow interpretation of its truth-seeking mandate: "Imagine that a truth commission had been appointed in the Soviet Union after Stalin, and this commission had said nothing about the Gulag. What credibility would it have had? The South African equivalent of the Gulag was called forced removals."[28] Indeed, the exclusion of such broad categories of human rights violations is not in conformity with Joinet's principles, which favor terms of reference that would give commissions the "jurisdiction to consider all forms of human rights violations."[29] Nonetheless, the act did give the TRC significant leeway in tasking it with painting a backdrop of the "antecedents, circumstances, factors and context of such violations, as well as the perspectives of the victims and the motives and perspectives of the persons responsible."[30] The Final Report speaks with eloquence about these "everyday" victimizations inherent in the apartheid system:

> Apartheid was a grim daily reality for every black South African. For at least 3.5 million black South Africans it meant collective expulsions, forced migration, bulldozing, gutting or seizure of homes, the mandatory carrying of passes, forced removals into rural ghettos and increased poverty and desperation. . . . One did not need to be a political activist to become a victim of apartheid; it was sufficient to be black, alive and seeking the basic necessities of life that whites took for granted and enjoyed by right.[31]

The arbitrariness of the mandate's cutoff dates for amnesty eligibility was highlighted by Parliament's subsequent decision to extend the eligibility period from December 6, 1993, to May 10, 1994. A certain degree of arbitrariness was inevitable in the South African context, because, as the Final Report notes, "racism came to South Africa in 1652."[32] What is perhaps more troubling, as discussed above, is that the TRC itself lobbied Parliament on behalf of extending its mandate period.

Impartiality and Independence

Hayner's call for "political backing but operational independence" for truth commissions complements the principle of "impartiality" Joinet specifies.[33] These elements—independence and impartiality—are combined under one benchmark because they address the same question from two different angles. Hayner points out that, to be effective, a truth commission must have official backing; this political backing sets the tone for the country's interaction with the truth commission. In addition, one can infer that this backing would translate, when appropriate, into operational support for the commission on the part of the goverment—for example, in facilitating access to government documents. But if a truth commission is to be credible, it must also have the freedom to exercise judgment, even on controversial political issues, free from influence—direct or indirect—from the government or any other major political players. But this logic presupposes impartiality— operational independence is rendered meaningless if the truth commission is not impartial to begin with and is not perceived to stay that way throughout the process.[34]

The TRC struggled with politics from day one, and it faced accusations of bias throughout its existence. A commendable vetting process for choosing the commissioners, besides facilitating public input, helped ensure that individual commissioners were reasonably impartial, but the selection process entailed no small amount of political horse-trading. Whether or not as a result of the commission's deliberate diversity, when the commissioners gathered around a table to make a decision, they often reverted to their "representative" roles, which was a recipe for paralysis.[35] Tutu and Boraine had the habit of saying that the commission was a microcosm of South African society and that any internal disputes were merely a reflection of that reality. But this excuse notwithstanding, the fact that certain commissioners were perceived—rightly or wrongly—as representing political or racial constituencies reinforced this problem and made individual commissioners and the TRC as a whole easy targets for criticism of this nature.

An anecdote about a meeting between TRC commissioners and President Mandela illustrates the integrity that Mandela brought to this equation, however. Consider this scenario. The top leadership of the TRC makes an appointment to meet with Mandela. When Mandela learns that de Klerk and Buthelezi, whose parties were both then partners in the GNU, have not been included in the meeting, he becomes quite upset. Mandela permits the group to stay for a nonsubstantive courtesy call, but he lets the commissioners know that in the future he will insist that the others be included in any meetings. "I want you to be independent. I don't want you to be anything other than independent," he is quoted as saying.[36]

That said, political parties did, with increasing frequency over the life span of the commission, try to exert pressure on the TRC, although they were usually savvy enough to do so indirectly.[37] Opportunistic leaks were apparently the favored vehicle for administering such pressure, and the media—some outlets more sensationally than others—often overplayed the political drama or controversy. It was not unheard of, particularly in the last act, for party representatives to pick up a telephone and call commissioners directly. But if commissioners and staff were not immune to political pressure, neither were they blameless. In one instance, commission representatives tried to exert political pressure on NGO representatives to call off a demonstration organized by victims to protest the nondelivery of reparations.[38] Neither was it unheard of for commissioners or staff members to leak internal TRC documents to the press.

For political parties, the TRC process represented an excuse for good old-fashioned political haymaking. As such, their politicking was not so much directed at infringing on the independence of the commission as it was at using the TRC to score political points. At some point not long into the commission's life, it became politically expedient for political parties to play to (if not foment) popular discontent with the TRC.[39] This culminated in the unseemly politics that surrounded the Final Report's public release, which proved, if nothing else, that the TRC was nobody's lackey. But at what cost to the long-term goal of reconciliation? The partisan nature of much of the parliamentary debate about the Final Report and the campaign politics in the run-up to the June 1999 elections also revealed this inclination. Of course, such vibrant interparty competition may be beneficial to and reflective of healthy democratic development, as long as it is manifested through nonviolent means. Indeed, the fact that the TRC was disparaged by all political parties served to contribute to its credibility as a body that was not subject to political influence. Although the issue cannot very well be addressed statutorily, future commissions may wish to consider how to tie the interests of political parties—usually focused on short-term political gain—to the long-term success of the commission.

Deliverables

Under this section, one might consider the TRC's end products and the extent to which they are likely to make a lasting, positive difference in the lives of individual South Africans and society at large. Simpson has commented about the danger, especially now that the Final Report has been released, that the TRC will be popularly perceived as nothing more than a vehicle for "putting the past behind us"; if that were the objective of the exercise, a blanket amnesty would have done the trick.[40] As its mandate made clear, the TRC had a much more ambitious agenda. So it is also important to consider the TRC's potential impact: How will society respond to the TRC process to move beyond the abusive past?

This discussion, then, not only considers the end products that the TRC has delivered—these have been, by and large, well conceived and well executed—but also takes into account the less than auspicious circumstances in which those deliverables have been rendered. Second, it should be acknowledged that the concept of "legacy" is laden with moral and political value judgments, and attempts at prognostication on what the commission's legacy will be are admittedly premature, if not presumptuous; only with the passage of time can one begin to tackle issues associated with the TRC's long-term societal impact. In the meantime, however, one might consider the quality of the TRC's deliverables and their short- to medium-term prospects. This study will confine itself to looking at the following end products that have come out of the TRC process: the Final Report, amnesty, and recommendations, including for reparations.

Reconciliation is an inherently long-term undertaking and has been, for this reason, purposefully excluded from this early assessment of deliverables.[41] Unfortunately, given the prominence of the "R word" in the act's title, in the name of the commission, and in public statements on all sides about the TRC agenda, expectations of instant or easily won reconciliation may have been raised.[42] Archbishop Tutu's liturgical style, coupled with his not infrequent public exhortations to victims to forgive perpetrators no doubt contributed to such perceptions.[43] Nonetheless, it would be unrealistic to anticipate that reconciliation would be an imme-diate outcome of the TRC, which was mandated to promote reconcilia-tion, not deliver it.

The Final Report. Mandated with compiling a "comprehensive report which sets out its activities and findings," the TRC obliged with a thirty-five-hundred-page, five-volume report.[44] As Hayner has pointed out, the Final Report itself is probably less important in South Africa, where the whole process has been characterized by "an amazing degree of transparency," compared with the final reports of truth commissions in most of the Latin American cases, where truth commissions operated behind closed doors.[45] Du Preez echoes this sentiment: "The real value of the Commission was in the process, in the telling of stories."[46] This observation certainly holds true in the short term, when memories of the TRC's often graphic hear-ings are still fresh. The Final Report and TRC archives will assume a more important role as these memories fade.

Has the Final Report established The Truth? As Krog points out, truth can have different meanings, and "each narrative carries the im-print of its narrator."[47] The TRC's mandate, wisely, was more nuanced: to establish "as complete a picture as possible."[48] The picture that emerges in the Final Report, which draws so heavily from the thou-sands of narratives given in testimony, is a monumental achievement. The Final Report does not pretend to provide an exhaustive docu-mentation. Rather, it presents a historical backdrop that credibly con-textualizes its thorough documentation of apartheid-era atrocities, both inside and outside South Africa. Complementing its depiction of the broad outlines and patterns of abuses, the Final Report highlights il-lustrative cases, drawn largely from the highly emotive human rights violations hearings.[49] Finally, excerpts from the thousands of com-pelling testimonies heard in various TRC hearings evoke the personal tragedies South Africans endured, allowing the reader to identify with the victims. Michael Ignatieff has written, "all that a truth commission can achieve is to reduce the number of lies that can be circulated un-challenged in public discourse."[50] And indeed, as a result of the TRC process and its documentation in the Final Report, it is no longer pos-sible to plausibly deny the nature or extent of atrocities that took place in apartheid South Africa.

In the Final Report, the TRC made numerous findings—designating victim status but also apportioning responsibility both in specific cases and for overall patterns of abuse. Most controversial are the "perpetrator findings," in which the TRC attributed moral or political responsibility based on the balance of probabilities. The TRC is not the first truth commission to name individuals and institutions found to be responsible for abuses. Nonetheless, du Toit raises concerns about the implications of these controversial findings, which are not grounded in due process and which, in his view, have questionable legal status.[51]

Despite the pitfalls that the absence of due process entailed, the TRC's perpetrator findings nonetheless have merit. To its credit, the TRC did, at a minimum, notify alleged perpetrators against whom it intended to make adverse findings and allow them an opportunity to respond in writing. Further, there was no pretense that these findings equated with a legal finding of guilt; rather, they were meant to impose moral punishment through the public shaming of perpetrators. Finally, the picture that the TRC was mandated to paint would have been far less complete had the commission not attempted to establish some level of accountability for the abuses that took place—not only for those who came forward to apply for amnesty for their actions, but also for those who shunned the amnesty process but who were no less guilty of perpetrating gross human rights violations. Indeed, the TRC would have been widely criticized had it not named names.

There are other shortcomings in the Final Report that warrant criticism. Several commentators have pointed out that it contains mistakes and inconsistencies.[52] Factual errors and inconsistencies are the regrettable, if understandable, product of the TRC's stretched resources and the realities of working under a tight production deadline.

Among the Final Report's imperfections are its often sketchy details about the commission's operations and decision-making process, especially on controversial decisions, as well as the lack of significant detail on the pros and cons of such.[53] A second shortcoming, which was emphasized by du Toit but which is well known to any researcher who has worked on the TRC, is the report's lack of an index and systematic cross-referencing.[54]

Finally, a word about the evenhandedness with which the report treated abuses on both sides of the apartheid struggle: to its credit, the TRC unapologetically applied the same standards of human rights across the board. At the same time, it was unequivocal that "those who fought against the system of apartheid were clearly fighting for a just cause, and those who sought to uphold and sustain apartheid cannot be morally equated with those who sought to remove and oppose it."[55] In maintaining its evenhandedness, the report occasionally lapsed into a language of moral absolutism that bordered on condescension, and it was this, perhaps, more than the judgments themselves, that so riled the ANC.[56]

Amnesty. As of December 1999, the Amnesty Committee had finalized 6,037 applications, with 815 outstanding.[57] Amnesty had been granted in full to 568 individuals and in part to 21. Of the remaining cases, 161 were withdrawn.[58] Over 640 were considered "not applicable" (that is, the acts were outside the TRC's jurisdiction). The vast majority of applications have been refused, the bulk on grounds of "no political objective," a criterion that has been applied without apparent bias to both ANC-aligned forces and members of the security forces.

There have been challenges to both the principle of granting amnesty and the TRC's process in doing so. First, the TRC was confronted with a "barrage of litigation" pertaining to the question of amnesty.[59] The families of Steve Biko and Griffiths Mxenge, along with the Azanian People's Organisation, challenged the constitutionality of the amnesty provisions that could deny them the right of filing civil suits against those responsible for killing their loved ones. As University of the Western Cape law professor Jeremy Sarkin noted, lack of clarity on the constitutionality of the act "saw the Amnesty Committee's work delayed pending resolution of the question."[60]

Second, everyone, it seems, was surprised that some 7,200 individuals applied for amnesty, and the Amnesty Committee was simply overwhelmed by the volume.[61] Once the Amnesty Committee had a full complement of staff and resources, it was better able to deliver with timely investigations and hearings, but the pressure to work through the backlog, according to Pigou, resulted in the fact that "the vast majority of amnesty applications [had] not been subjected to an investigative process of any sort."[62] Kader Asmal et al. faulted the commission for not interpreting its mandate in such a way that perpetrators would have to apologize for their actions in order to receive amnesty.[63] On the other hand, Marius Schoon, whose wife and daughter were blown up by a parcel bomb sent by security force agents, objected strenuously to the "crocodile tears" proffered by Craig Williamson, one of the perpetrators of that act.[64] Many victims also complained about the short turnaround time faced by perpetrators who received amnesty, compared to the victims' own lengthy (and ongoing) wait for reparations.

Objections to the very notion of amnesty have persisted. Critics argue that, aside from contributing to an atmosphere of impunity, amnesty lends an aura of legitimacy to the heinous acts that were committed in the name of apartheid, revictimizes the survivors of horrific acts, and risks debasing the whole society in the process. A growing sense of repugnance on the part of South African people—particularly victims—toward the notion of granting amnesty to perpetrators left Tutu on the defensive: "We did not decide on amnesty. The political parties decided on amnesty."[65] His comments reflect an interesting dynamic that developed in this context: for the most part, political parties escaped criticism for the amnesty provision to which they agreed. Instead, such criticism was directed primarily at the TRC.

Recommendations and Reparations. The TRC was specifically tasked with making recommendations regarding "the creation of institutions conducive to a stable and fair society and the institutional administrative and legislative measures" required to prevent human rights violations, as well as the "granting of reparation to victims or the taking of other measures aimed at rehabilitating and restoring the human and civil dignity of victims."[66] It is useful to consider both the appropriateness of the TRC's recommendations and the likelihood that they will be implemented.

Turning first to those recommendations that concern reparations, one should acknowledge that the TRC's recommended reparations regime is tempered by a greater degree of realism vis-à-vis budgetary and political constraints than are the Joinet principles.[67] For example, Joinet asserts the victim's right to and the state's duty to make reparations for "any human

rights violation," compensation for which "must equal the financially as-
sessable value of all damage suffered."[68] Among other things, the Joinet
principles include similarly worded provisions for rehabilitative measures,
such as medical or psychological care, and measures of collective reparation, such as commemorative ceremonies and monuments. Apartheid's
legacy of widespread poverty necessitated that the TRC's recommended
reparations package be tempered with fiscal realism. As the Final Report
noted:

> The plight of those who, through the legacy of apartheid, need assis-
> tance in the form of social spending (for housing, education, health care
> and so on) must also be remembered. The provision of reparations to
> the (relatively) few victims of gross human rights violations who ap-
> peared before the Commission cannot be allowed to prejudice
> apartheid's many other victims. The need to provide reparations for the
> former cannot be allowed to constitute so great a drain on the national
> fiscus that insufficient resources remain for essential social upliftment
> and reconstruction programmes.[69]

Joinet also refers to the right of victims to "a readily available,
prompt and effective remedy in the form of criminal, civil, and
administrative or disciplinary proceedings," which, given the TRC's
amnesty provisions, the commission obviously cannot deliver.[70] Aside
from these gaps, which are all attributable to political compromise or
budgetary realism, one should recognize that the government and
Parliament share the blame for the considerable lag time that has characterized the actual delivery of reparations. That the first payments of
"urgent interim reparations" were not made until July 1998, for example, is appalling. When contrasted with the short turnaround that perpetrators faced in receiving amnesty, the seemingly interminable wait
for reparations not only skewed the balance upon which the TRC was
crafted but eroded goodwill on the part of victims toward both the government and the TRC.

To its credit, the TRC was also cognizant of its obligations to promote less quantifiable but equally important vehicles of reparations.
For example, in response to the numerous reports of unsolved "disappearances," the TRC investigated and in over fifty cases was able to
locate secret graves, identify remains, and turn them over to families
for proper burial.[71] In addition, the TRC recommended numerous

measures to ensure that such human rights abuses as took place in the past do not recur in the future.

Depending on how one counts them, there are about 250 separate recommendations in the Final Report.[72] Unfortunately, the quantity of the recommendations is not always matched by their quality. Some, for example, are so vaguely worded that they risk trivializing the exercise. What does the TRC mean, for example, when it recommends that "the Government must ensure that the rule of law, human rights practice, transparency, accountability and the rooting out of corruption and other forms of criminality at all levels of society *are seriously addressed*" (emphasis mine)?[73] Neither is it always clear to whom the recommendations are directed. Although it may serve a useful purpose to use the passive voice—and thus avoid finger-pointing—the recommendation, for example, that "strategies be devised for reintegrating perpetrators into society" does not easily lend itself to implementation or accountability.[74] Other recommendations reflect an expansive interpretation of the mandate, seemingly overstepping the bounds of preventing human rights violations. One might ask, for example, how the following assertion falls within the TRC mandate: "If organised crime is to be combated, those involved in crime syndicates will have to come forward. This is only likely if such persons are assured of comprehensive witness protection."[75] Finally, those recommendations that are accompanied by a brief explanation or rationale are significantly more useful than those that are not.[76]

That said, one could argue that if a commission is to err in making recommendations, it is probably better to err on the side of too many rather than too few, and on an expansive rather than minimalist interpretation of the appropriate scope of the recommendations. In the South African case, at least, the pervasive legacy of apartheid may justify such an approach. The majority of the TRC's recommendations reflect a well-thought-through response to both the glaring needs for societal transformation and more practical needs—particularly those of victims—that became apparent in the TRC process.

Whether these recommendations are implemented is, of course, another matter. The degree to which implementation is carried out is not only a function of political will, which would be hard to muster in any case, given that the recommendations are not prioritized and most carry a high price tag. Even in the best of circumstances, there would be fierce competition for South Africa's scarce resources, which are just as much needed to redress gaps in the provision of basic services for South Africa's black population, the majority of whom would not qualify for victim status (and thereby reparations grants) under the act. As discussed above, sensitivity to this dilemma is at least partly responsible for the reluctance on the part of some ANC politicians to allocate money to implement the TRC's recommended individual reparations grants. But the dynamics of the hostile political climate that accompanied the finalization of the Final Report have exacerbated what would already have been bleak prospects for implementation, not only for those recommendations dealing with reparations, but for the whole body of recommendations. For example, some observers have expressed concern that the South African government does not appear to be receptive to be the TRC's recommendations that all commission records be transferred to the National Archives when the codicil to the Final Report is made public, and that such records be made accessible to the public.[77]

Similarly, despite Mandela's rejection of a blanket amnesty, the ANC's continued flirtation with the notion (de facto, if not de jure; "group," if not "blanket") is contrary to the TRC's recommendation that "in order to avoid a culture of impunity and to entrench the rule of law, the granting of a general amnesty *in whatever guise* should be resisted" (emphasis mine).[78] Indeed, as argued above, a general amnesty would make a mockery of the whole TRC process. Even a more narrowly defined "collective amnesty" risks undermining the moral basis on which the TRC process was built. To the extent that the example of the TRC and the lessons learned from it are studied by the architects of (and participants in) future truth commissions—and there are a variety of reasons why the TRC might be taken, not as a blueprint, certainly, but as a model nonetheless—one should consider the possible implications for those future commissions if South Africa fails to prosecute those against whom solid cases could be built, who were denied amnesty, or who did not even apply.

Neil Kritz, noted scholar of transitional justice mechanisms, has expressed the opinion, for example, that the failure to prosecute such perpetrators in South Africa would effectively emasculate future truth commissions should they adopt the South African model's carrot and stick of amnesty for full disclosure and the threat of prosecutions against those who do not come forward.[79] Absent the leverage offered by the credible threat of prosecution, perpetrators would be emboldened to eschew the amnesty process, with potentially disastrous consequences for the effort of establishing as many facts as possible about the past and of holding perpetrators accountable for their actions in at least some nominal fashion. And if the threat of political instability (let alone political expediency) can be wielded to effectively stymie prosecutions in a society that had all the benefits that South Africa had, including a well-established rule of law and a functioning (if flawed) judicial system, one need only imagine what the prospects of prosecution might be in societies without these benefits. Clearly, however, these potential ramifications are not foremost on the minds of those responsible for making decisions on the question of whom (if anyone) should be prosecuted in South Africa.[80]

Of course, some recommendations will carry less of a political cost than others, and these may face better prospects. Many of the recommendations are directed at nongovernmental actors, such as faith communities, the media, and the business sector. For example, the TRC recommended that "religious communities organize ceremonies designed to enable people to acknowledge their different levels of involvement in the human rights violations of the past" and that "religious communities explore the possibility of joining with other organisations of civil society in setting up trauma centers and counselling initiatives."[81] And while the TRC, or the government for that matter, has little leverage with which to effect the implementation of such recommendations, it does not hurt to make them. The NGO sector will play a key role in the follow-up stage, particularly in performing advocacy and watchdog functions regarding the implementation of the majority of recommendations, which are directed at governmental bodies. Here, South Africa is in excellent hands.

LOGISTICAL BENCHMARKS

Administration

Under this rubric, in addition to considering management issues, one might combine two separate guidelines from Hayner: "time and resources for preparation and set up" and "appropriate funding and staffing."[82] The commission benefited from significant advantages.

Interested South Africans had done their homework, which was reflected in a well-crafted mandate. The TRC also had considerable resources, in terms of both human capital and funding. At its height, the TRC had approximately four hundred staff members. This compares with El Salvador's thirty-strong commission, Chile's staff of sixty, and the two hundred persons who staffed the Guatemalan Historical Clarification Commission.[83] In terms of funding, the TRC's total operating budget consisted of allocations from the South African government's budget, which amounted to R165 million (about $27.5 million, or about $9 million a year), and foreign donations amounting to over R31 million (about $5 million, or an additional $1.7 million per year).[84] By comparison, the El Salvadoran commission's annual budget was $2.5 million and the Chilean commission's was closer to $1 million.[85]

Why, then, one might ask, were there chronic administrative problems? In its Final Report, the TRC asserts that one of its greatest challenges was the absence of a provision for a start-up period, such as Hayner recommends, during which "offices could be located and established, staff sought and appointed, and a modus operandi carefully developed. There was little time for reflection."[86] This sentiment was echoed by the secretary of the Amnesty Committee, who, when asked what, if anything, he would recommend be done differently, said, "there should be a considerable time period in which to prepare for what will be forthcoming. . . . if you had the full complement of ninety-nine people in place two years ago, I think we would have been finished by now."[87] Similarly, Fazel Randera said, "if I were to act as an adviser to any grouping wanting to set up a truth commission, regardless of the pressure that society puts on us, that commission should take at least six months working out the parameters and process that they would follow, including trying to set up the proper structures."[88] While one can sympathize with the need for such a preparatory period and recognize the negative consequences the TRC suffered for lack of one, it should also be acknowledged that the political climate at the time of the TRC's formation did exert considerable pressure on the new commission to begin delivering results immediately.[89]

The TRC can perhaps be forgiven, then, for the ad-hocism that characterized its day-to-day operations in the early stages; what is perhaps more troubling is that that ad-hocism was not confined to the early stages.

There were also serious information flow problems within the commission, particularly between investigators and researchers: "The pace was too quick for the Research Unit to share information, the most important task."[90] One commissioner described the management of the TRC as a "nightmare," commenting that the chief executive officer did not exert his authority, which left a power vacuum that some commissioners routinely exploited to circumvent the formal policymaking process.[91] A staff member described the TRC's policy formulation process thus: "Typically, there would be two or three or four crises, and then we would realize that we needed a policy."[92] As time went on, the TRC seemed to be plagued with one crisis after another, including a steady stream of litigation. As a result, the TRC operated in crisis mode much of the time, with predictable consequences for long-term management. No less predictable was the result that, in the words of one TRC staffer, "sometimes we tread on victims' toes."[93] Imagine how a victim might feel, for example, upon learning—from the media, not the TRC—that the perpetrator responsible for killing a loved one had received amnesty.

Some have suggested that the TRC's seeming managerial deficit was largely a function of having two ministers at the helm. In exploring this line of thinking, one should not discount that both Tutu and Boraine had impeccable credentials in terms of moral integrity. The TRC could well have faltered without such strong moral leadership. Krog characterized Tutu as the compass of the commission: "The process is unthinkable without Tutu. Impossible."[94] Krog noted, however, that there was considerable baggage associated with his ecclesiastical leadership style: "Tutu from the beginning unambiguously mantled the Commission in Christian language. . . . he finds it difficult to move from the strong hierarchy of the Church to the democracy of the Commission."[95] In retrospect, therefore, one might question the legislation's stipulation that commissioners be vetted on the basis of their political suitability and moral integrity, without any comparable managerial litmus test. Indeed, the very vetting process for commissioners, which seemingly valued representivity over all else, led to bottlenecks on difficult policy questions. It is interesting to recall Zalaquett's advice in this regard: "There may sometimes be a tension between ideal representativeness and quality. One should try to have both but if this is not possible it is preferable to sacrifice the perfect balance for the sake of quality."[96] If one accepts the frequently proffered excuse that, as a microcosm of broader South African society, the TRC reflected that society's tensions and difficulties, that hardly bodes well for the future, because it is that society that is expected to act on the TRC's work.

Finally, the TRC's operating budget was allocated as a separate line item out of the Department of Justice's budget, as approved by Parliament on a fiscal-year basis. One might ask how this squares with Hayner's urging that "the question of continued funding cannot be used, or be perceived to be used, as a point of leverage to influence the Commission's work."[97] Although there is no indication that the government tried to leverage the TRC's revenues for influence, the Final Report is clear that "the Commission operated under strained financial conditions virtually all the time."[98] The TRC turned to foreign and domestic donor funding to help make up the shortfall, but in the interim budgetary constraints forced the TRC to make financial compromises that proved costly, for example, in terms of its investigative capacity. As mentioned above, the failure on the part of government and Parliament to promptly authorize disbursement for reparations is particularly troubling.

Given the immense workload set out in the TRC's mandate, coupled with the limited resources to which the commission had access, it is fair to ask whether the TRC could have completed its task any sooner. On this question, one might defer to the self-critical judgment of one of the commissioners, who acknowledged that "there were managers who did not always apply themselves, and commissioners and staff whose skills were underutilized."[99] It would be a mistake, then, to place the blame for delays solely on the lack of necessary resources.

The cumulative political impact of these administrative problems and resulting delays should not be understated. Wasted time and resources in the commission's early stages meant that the TRC lost many of the benefits associated with the new South Africa's honeymoon period, including a certain degree of momentum and goodwill on the part of the South African people. With each extension of its life span, the TRC came closer and closer to campaign season. Rather than being viewed as the product of the transition, the TRC came to be viewed instead as an element of political stalemate. *New York Times* reporter Suzanne Daley addressed this dynamic: "The Commission is finishing its work long after the euphoria of a peaceful transition has worn thin. . . . The report is landing just as the country is gearing up for what promises to be a vicious and combative election year."[100]

Safeguards

This category encompasses two of Joinet's principles that address a truth commission's protective obligations vis-à-vis victims, witnesses, and perpetrators. Victims and witnesses may be endangered and perpetrators (or alleged perpetrators) may be implicated as the truth comes out in the course of human rights violations hearings or the investigatory process. With regard to alleged perpetrators, Joinet stipulates both that, in the process of establishing the truth about past abuses, the commission should attempt to corroborate the information it gathers, and that persons implicated in past abuses should have the opportunity to make statements or submit relevant documentation setting out their versions of the facts.[101] The TRC's investigative unit, made up of sixty local investigators and twelve specialists from foreign police services, fulfilled the corroborative requirement, though it did not always do so in the most efficient manner or without controversy.[102]

The act addressed the obligations toward implicated persons by affording them "an opportunity to submit representations to the Commission within a specified time . . . or to give evidence at a hearing of the Commission."[103] Many observers have bemoaned the "legalization" of the TRC process (that is, the way in which the process came to be dominated by legal questions) that resulted from too rigorous a protection of the interests of perpetrators rather than from the act itself. Sarkin has pointed out, however, that had the act been submitted to the Constitutional Court for abstract review before it came into operation, the constitutional challenges could have been avoided, and that even absent that review, the TRC could have avoided much of the costly legal wrangling if it been more attentive to the long-term ramifications of the legal issues at play.[104] Finally, with respect to protecting perpetrators, the act provides that, in the event of the Amnesty Committee's refusal to grant amnesty, "no adverse inference shall be drawn by the court."[105]

With regard to the need to protect victims and witnesses who endanger themselves in coming forward with the truth, Joinet asserts, though without elaboration, that truth commissions should guarantee the security and protection of witnesses and victims.[106] The TRC deserves credit as the first truth commission to provide for a witness protection program (WPP) to meet this need.[107] The TRC appointed former KwaZulu-Natal deputy attorney-general Chris Macadam to head the program. Despite its limited budget, over 150 individuals were able to take advantage of this program. The Final Report outlines three categories of people who approached the WPP for assistance:

▶ victims who were afraid of being targeted by vigilante groups;
▶ potential witnesses who feared for their safety and security should they disclose what they knew or had done; and
▶ confidence tricksters who, often motivated by financial enrichment, wished to mislead the commission by falsely professing knowledge of cases under investigation.[108]

Rigorous admission criteria helped screen out those who fell into the third category. Noncompliance with these criteria could also result in termination of WPP services. Thus, the criteria had the benefit of affording the TRC some measure of control over those potential witnesses who might otherwise have used the program for nefarious ends. When the security risk was assessed as low to moderate, the TRC employed community-based protection, which allowed witnesses to stay in their own homes. In some cases, the TRC assigned witness protectors to guard the witnesses in their homes. In higher-risk cases, witnesses were placed in safe houses.

Despite the fact that the WPP suffered from chronic funding shortfalls, it deserves credit for some important successes. In particular, the Final Report makes note of the ripple effect of one well-executed case:

> A senior member of the security police compound at Vlakplaas was persuaded to make a complete disclosure. His statements, particularly as regards secret orders issued by generals, were passed on to the Investigation Unit and made a major impact on section 29 inquiries. As a direct and immediate result of this disclosure, a group of former security officers headed by an ex-director decided to "come clean" and were debriefed by the Witness Protection Unit. . . . Consequently, the following cases were solved: the disappearance and murder of Madaka and Mthimkulu; "the PEBCO Three"; the "Cradock Four"; Steve Biko; Kondile and Mkhuseli Jack.[109]

5

EXTRAPOLATING FROM THE TRC

The purpose of the above stock-taking exercise is twofold. First, even a preliminary assessment may offer significant indicators as policymakers ponder the extent to which truth commissions offer a viable means for dealing with past chronic abuses. It is too early to predict with any certainty what kind of staying power truth commissions will have for societies that are grappling with these issues. But, given that there are several countries in which some variation of the idea is currently being contemplated, it is safe to assume that new models will continue to emerge, at least in the short to medium term.[1] Second, to the extent that such mechanisms offer a viable alternative to transitioning societies wrestling with the tough questions associated with abuse, accountability, and justice, it is hoped that post mortem assessments can contribute to an awareness of the kinds of political obstacles such mechanisms may face, and be of benefit in ongoing policy debates about how to make such bodies more effective in the future. South Africa benefited from a well-greased learning curve on truth commissions, and this study now turns to some of the key lessons learned from the TRC process that might benefit other countries contemplating truth commissions. Embodying this spirit of constructive criticism, Boraine commented: "We had insights into the strengths and especially the weaknesses of other efforts. I hope others will learn from our weaknesses, because I think we made some mistakes."[2]

CONDUCIVE ENVIRONMENT

To start with, it is useful to consider some of the aspects of the South African sociopolitical context that were conducive to or positively informed the TRC process. Without suggesting that such factors assume sine qua non status with regard to future truth commissions, one can nonetheless make the case that a truth commission's prospects may be enhanced to the extent that such aspects are manifest.

▶ *Critical Mass.* Throughout the TRC process, there existed in South African society and among its political forces sufficient support behind the objective of the process to sustain the commission—this despite a myriad of legal and other challenges. One might first consider the relative balance of power between the former apartheid regime and the former liberation-movement–turned–democratically-elected-government. Clearly, "victor's justice" in the form of Nuremberg-type trials in South Africa was not an option in the face of a threatened right-wing insurrection. But neither would the ANC have been prepared to accept a self-amnesty on the part of the former regime. That the TRC developed out of the process of a negotiated settlement between former adversaries is reflected in many of the compromises that shaped the TRC's mandate, most notably the amnesty provision in the post-amble to the Interim Constitution. That the power balance shifted over time is clear when one looks at the many provisions that were subsequently introduced to the TRC legislation, in particular, those that were concerned with truth seeking and accountability, as well as reparations. Once the TRC was operational, the dynamics continued to evolve; the upswing in party political bickering that accompanied the NP's withdrawal from the GNU to become an opposition party is an illustration of this point. In the face of these evolving political realities, there remained a core constituency that supported the TRC. The idea here is not to suggest that South Africa's political power dynamics offer a blueprint. But there is some value in considering whether, in future scenarios, a critical mass exists among people who have political (and military) power and who are in favor of a truth commission and will support it, participate in it, and be willing to pay a political cost for it. On the flip side, one might consider the availability of appropriate mechanisms to help keep in check those who might be inclined to undermine or stymie a truth commission. Some of the following aspects that contributed to a permissive environment in South Africa address the latter issue.

▶ *Civil Society.* Perhaps most importantly, South Africa had the advantage of a strong civil society, made up of individuals and institutions whose skills were honed through many years of contesting apartheid. A plethora of NGOs and community-based organizations had long been engaged at the grassroots level in activities such as investigating and compiling data to document human rights violations; challenging the apartheid system through the court system, public campaigns and demonstrations, and human rights education; and providing legal and other assistance to victims of human rights abuses. As discussed above, many such groups contributed to the conceptualization and indeed the legislation of the TRC, and they also provided oversight during the TRC's life span. These same NGOs, and a new one under the leadership of Villa-Vicencio, will be critical in carrying out a watchdog function, both monitoring the government's response to the TRC's recommendations and performing an advocacy role, especially if the government's response is deemed inadequate. That the TRC failed to take full advantage of NGO networks—particularly in the areas of victim outreach and post-trauma counseling—represents a missed opportunity that future commissions would be well advised to remedy.

▶ *Independent Media.* Second, the existence of a strong and independent media has been a tremendous advantage to the TRC process. Intense media scrutiny, it can be argued, helped mitigate the fallibility of the commission. As discussed above, public hearings created an environment conducive to the widespread media coverage that accompanied the process. And if, as some have argued, the existence of TV cameras at hearings was responsible for the TRC's degeneration into a "Kleenex commission," as it was derisively called, that is perhaps an acceptable cost of the unprecedented transparency the media contributed to the process. This media attention resulted in public awareness of, scrutiny of, and debate about the TRC process. This, despite the fact that some of the media coverage was slanted—the Afrikaans press, in particular, was often gratuitously vindictive toward the TRC—and tended to sensationalize conflicts associated with the TRC. Finally, while it may have been disappointing to those who support the idea of truth commissions, it is hardly surprising that a variety of actors would try to use the media as a vehicle to manipulate perceptions about the commission, if not the commission itself. The existence of competing and independent media outlets helped to keep this practice in check.

▶ *Functioning Judicial System.* In addition, South Africa came to the table with a functioning judicial system, something that cannot be taken for granted in most transitioning societies. This had a practical effect on the South African model, for example, in that the TRC had a pool of experienced judges from which to draw for its Amnesty Committee. In addition, the TRC relied on the threat of criminal prosecution in that judicial system as an inducement for perpetrators to apply for amnesty. This is not to suggest that the new South Africa's inherited legal system left nothing to be desired. As the Final Report states, many in the legal profession—including many of its judges and magistrates—were complicit in lending apartheid "the aura of legitimacy" and contributed to "the entrenchment and defense of apartheid through the courts."[3] There did exist, nonetheless, a strong basis for the rule of law under the new dispensation. In the absence of the rule of law, the public might not have had confidence in a quasi-judicial process, such as the amnesty process, let alone the judicial system itself.

▶ *Moral Leadership.* Finally, it is worth acknowledging that, throughout this process, South Africa has had the unparalleled advantage of Nelson Mandela's moral leadership. The importance of this advantage should not be understated, though it would be patently unfair to hold other societies to such a standard. Tutu has referred to Mandela as "an icon of reconciliation."[4] Indeed, Mandela embodied the spirit of reconciliation, and he articulated a vision for national unity, reconciliation, and societal transformation with which South Africans of all backgrounds could identify. In so doing, he set an amazing example not only for South Africans but for the world. At the same time, South Africa was fortunate to have had individuals with the impeccable credentials and moral authority of Archbishop Desmond Tutu and Alex Boraine to lead the TRC and set the tone for the process.

TRANSLATING CONCEPTS INTO PRACTICE

The TRC scores high marks for its well-conceived mandate. But any commission whose mandate includes such lofty principles as promoting "national unity and reconciliation in a spirit of understanding which transcends the conflicts and divisions of the past" is bound to encounter difficulty in giving those ideals practical effect.[5] Because future commissions will likely face similar difficulties, it is useful to consider briefly the TRC's experience in grappling with the conceptual tensions inherent in such ideals.

▶ *Justice vs. Reconciliation.* Truth commissions—especially if they are accompanied by an amnesty provision—are often compared unfavorably to strictly judicial accountability mechanisms, whether domestic or international. Human rights advocates tend to favor prosecution of perpetrators of gross human rights violations and criticize truth commissions for sacrificing justice in pursuit of truth, reconciliation, and/or peace. Unpalatable and morally repugnant though political compromise may be, this study has accepted as a given the compromise that resulted in the TRC's amnesty concession. This book does not attempt to resolve the moral, legal, political, or philosophical dilemmas posed by an amnesty regime. These arguments are well articulated in the extensive body of literature on the subject.[6] Rather, this book has examined some of the political ramifications associated with the South African model, which wisely couples amnesty with a strenuous truth-seeking and accountability function. It is worth acknowledging, however, that the relative costs and benefits of justice, truth, and reconciliation have been hotly debated in South Africa, as they have been in other countries that have experimented with truth and reconciliation commissions. Such questions are sure to be revisited wherever future truth commissions crop up.

For example, in bringing a court challenge against the constitutionality of the TRC's amnesty process, the Azanian People's Organisation, along with the Biko and Mxenge families, made a compelling case against the state's right to indemnify the killers of their loved ones. Not only did the case strike "at the heart of the Amnesty

Committee's very existence," as the Final Report commented; it represented a fundamental challenge to the TRC as a whole.[7] Ultimately, although then Constitutional Court judge Ismail Mahomed, who authored the court's judgment in this case, indicated that he sympathized with the families' desire to see the perpetrators vigorously prosecuted and punished for their callous and inhumane conduct, the court upheld the constitutionality of the amnesty provision.[8]

Should the government undertake a post-TRC collective amnesty, that initiative, too, will likely be subjected to a constitutional test. As stated above, that such an initiative is even being considered by the government underscores the lesson that transitioning societies should be on guard against the political expediency of amnesty programs. To the extent that future truth commissions successfully meet the objective benchmarks discussed above, they will be not only better equipped to withstand political and legal challenges that arise in their respective domestic contexts but also better prepared to defend their actions against those who may have recourse to extraterritorial accountability processes—whether through extradition to another country's national courts, as in the Pinochet case, or under the auspices of the ICC.[9]

▶ *The Doctrine of Evenhandedness.* In retrospect, it is interesting to note that the word "evenhandedness" is not used in the act; clearly, however, the commissioners concluded that it would smack of bias if they did not hold agents of the government and members of the liberation movements to the same objective standards of human rights. Importantly, the TRC distinguished between evenhandedness and moral equivalence, notwithstanding the ANC's protestations to the contrary. Indeed, the Final Report explicitly rejected moral equivalence, endorsed the view that apartheid constituted a crime against humanity, and made a "primary finding" against the apartheid state.[10] This issue was particularly sensitive in the South African context because of the ANC's strongly held belief that the struggle against apartheid constituted a "just war," a perception both echoed and fueled by the international community's condemnation of apartheid as a crime against humanity.[11] In addition, the ANC is the only liberation movement to have explicitly embraced the Geneva conventions, a move that gave it considerable moral high ground over a government that not only abrogated its duty to protect its citizens from such abuse but actively oppressed the majority of them. Not all liberation movements are as conscientious as was the ANC in trying to adhere to international norms and standards of human rights; nonetheless, the politics of evenhandedness will likely pose difficulties wherever future truth commissions are mandated to examine a past in which atrocities have not been confined to one side in a conflict. In making the politically loaded judgments about how to handle the relative responsibility of the different parties—whether they are government agents, paramilitaries, members of liberation movements, or guerrillas—future truth commissions would do well to heed Tutu's advice that "it would be the height of stupidity as well as being self-defeating for the Commission to subvert its work by being anything less than fair and even-handed."[12]

▶ *Victim-Friendly Orientation.* To the extent that future commissions follow the TRC's lead in incorporating principles for dealing with victims, it may also be useful to consider some pitfalls the TRC faced in realizing those principles. In spite of the TRC's exemplary victim-centered mandate, much of the TRC process ended up being guided by its legal obligations to perpetrators. The resulting legalization of the process was hardly victim-friendly. And to the extent that there is a significant portion of the population that passively benefited from the policies of the former repressive regime, future truth commissions would do well to avoid focusing on victims and perpetrators to the exclusion of beneficiaries. In addition, as discussed above, the TRC was hamstrung by a mandate that reserved for the government, in consultation with Parliament, the power to make final decisions on disbursement of reparations to victims, which would have represented the most tangible evidence of the supposed victim-friendly orientation. The rationale behind political intervention in such decisions is discussed above. The reluctance to compensate some victims at the expense of others is likely to be replicated in other societies. One possible solution might be to incorporate in the reparations package a system that would give designated victims of gross human rights violations priority in making claims before other bodies that the successor regime might have in place to help redress the more general poverty and basic needs issues.[13] Such a system could also incorporate a means test to ensure that assistance to victims of gross human rights violations does not unfairly displace assistance directed at the more generally disadvantaged.[14] Both of these tools were considered and rejected in the South African context, but they might be more appropriate in other scenarios.

Aside from recommending a reparations package that was apparently perceived as too costly given available resources, one other unforeseen consequence of the TRC's victim-friendly approach was an inclination on the part of the TRC to be generous in designating victim status to those who came forward to make statements.[15] Individuals would not be eligible for any reparations without a TRC "victim finding" that they had been subjected to a gross human rights violation. The bureaucratic correlative of this approach was that, when the perpetrator of the act for which the victim was recognized as such was known, that person (or group of persons or organization) automatically would be designated by a "perpetrator finding" as being responsible for a gross human rights violation.[16] Thus the desire to compensate the victim—even in a situation, for example, when a victim is caught in a crossfire between guerrillas and police forces—resulted in a finding against the perpetrators, in this case, those engaged in the shooting. The ANC's objections to the findings against it in the Final Report stemmed in large part from this automatic linkage between victim status and perpetrator findings.

CONCLUSION

Victims of human rights abuse, advocates of human rights, scholars, and interested parties in other countries undergoing a transition from repressive regimes to democratic governance will likely study the South African TRC for applicable features. Donors who will be asked to provide financial and other support to future commissions will doubtlessly consider the extent to which the South African model provided a good return on donors' investments and whether it is a model worthy of replication. Meanwhile, those who have played or who will assume political roles in societies contemplating truth commissions might be most interested in the bottom-line political significance of such an exercise. This study has not tried to argue that the TRC offers a blueprint in any of these respects. Rather, to the extent that the TRC represents something of a harbinger for the direction future truth commissions—assuming they are not just a fad—might take, this study has attempted to examine the TRC process, and in particular some of its more politically controversial aspects, for potentially applicable insights and lessons learned, including an analysis of the political dynamics at play and the way in which they contributed to or detracted from the TRC process and its long-term objectives. As stated above, it would be premature to attempt to assess the end result at this stage, but it is not too early to begin taking stock of the process and considering the potential implications.

Praising the TRC process as "enormously successful," Justice Richard Goldstone of the Constitutional Court opined that "history will judge it as a very important process."[1] The correctness of Goldstone's assessment can be seen in the many achievements of which the TRC can boast. Probably its most enduring accomplishment is that it offered an accessible platform from which ordinary victims of political violence could tell their stories and receive a sympathetic hearing. Thanks to the saturation media coverage they received, these compelling stories profoundly altered the public's awareness about the nature and extent of abuses that took place under apartheid. These stories—and the people who told them—have earned their place in South Africa's history books. The picture painted in the course of victim testimonies was largely corroborated in the amnesty process, whose public hearings featuring perpetrators of heinous crimes detailing their actions and motivations also generated intense public discourse. It was in the amnesty process that it became apparent just how high a price society was paying for the truth. But that was part of the bargain—the negotiated settlement. As one evaluates the value of the exercise, one should contemplate the unrest, vigilantism, or civil war that might have ensued in the absence of the TRC.

Nonetheless, the report card in chapter 4 shows clear room for improvement. Some of the disappointment with the TRC can be attributed to the unrealistic expectations that some people had of what it could achieve. Indeed, many of the TRC's problems were largely a function of competing priorities: different constituencies had distinct aspirations for the commission that were not necessarily mutually reinforcing. A truth commission that tries to be all things to all people will ultimately disappoint everyone. Like most critiques of the South African process, this one pertains as much to the TRC's mandate, and the politicians who crafted it, as it does to the commission itself and the sociopolitical environment in which it played out. Much, of course, will depend on what South African society does with the recommendations put forward by the TRC.

In this regard, it is worth revisiting a piece of advice that Jose Zalaquett shared with South African interlocutors at one of the pre-TRC consultative conferences. Zalaquett was commenting on the sequence of events in Argentina, where, following the work of that country's National Commission on the Disappearance of Persons, the state successfully prosecuted several junta members responsible for disappearances in the "dirty war" (including two former presidents, in addition to chiefs of police and military generals), but the military pressed Argentine president Alfonsin into adopting amnesty laws, and Alfonsin's successor, President Menem, subsequently pardoned those junta members who had been convicted. "It is worse for a political leader who enjoys legitimacy to have to go back on what he proposed than to achieve less than would have been ideal. In Argentina the president aimed too high. As a result he faced a backlash and had to put the stamp of a democratic president on ugly impunity measures."[2] The question of whether and whom to prosecute—among those who were denied amnesty and those who did not even bother to apply for it—now faces the South African government. The decisions the South African government makes on these questions—and whether any "ugly impunity measures" are subsequently adopted—will have enormous consequences in South Africa and perhaps in future scenarios, as well.

A final note on the politics of the TRC: truth commissions are not only concerned with the past; they are just as much about the future. The South African TRC is no exception. Given the high stakes involved, it is hardly surprising that political haymaking accompanied the TRC process. It will be critical, however, for those who wish to advance the truth and reconciliation process to work together and move beyond the acrimony that was epitomized by the politics surrounding the release of the Final Report. It is hoped that the postelection political climate will be more conducive to that goal, but it is not at all clear that the political parties have an exit strategy in hand. It may fall, then, to nonpartisan NGOs and community-based organizations to jump-start this process. Clearly, the work has just begun if South Africa is to fully realize the "once in a lifetime/ . . . longed-for tidal wave/of justice," where "hope and history rhyme," about which Seamus Heaney wrote in *The Cure at Troy*.

NOTES

1. INTRODUCTION

1. The five-volume *Truth and Reconciliation Commission of South Africa Report* (hereafter referred to as the Final Report) was handed over to President Mandela at a nationally televised ceremony on October 29, 1998, and was released to the public the same day. (Although the document was billed as the "Final Report," the TRC's Amnesty Committee is not expected to finalize its work until the latter part of 2000. The Amnesty Committee will produce a codicil to the Final Report at that time.) There was widespread media coverage of the event and the last-minute court challenges launched by both former president F. W. de Klerk and the African National Congress. Unless otherwise stated, quotations were recorded by the author, who attended the event, or are from published texts of speeches.

2. I discuss the politics of these court challenges in greater detail later in this study. Although the handover ceremony was not derailed, as was threatened, the atmosphere was significantly soured. As Suzanne Daley wrote in the *New York Times* on October 30, 1999, "far from being the salve for South Africa's wounds that some had hoped it would be, the Truth and Reconciliation Commission's final report on this country's brutal past was released Thursday in the bitter atmosphere of court challenges and political bickering."

3. Familiar themes included the TRC as circus, as witch hunt, and as an institution lacking in credibility. Ironically, those who had disparaged the TRC for being the lackey of the ANC did not seem to appreciate the significance of the TRC's resoluteness in fighting the ANC court challenge.

4. Consider, for example, DP delegate Peter Leon's comment: "The reactions of the ANC have been like Tweedledum and Tweedledee" (*Star,* November 18, 1998).

5. Particularly noteworthy in the comparative literature are three volumes edited by Neil Kritz, *Transitional Justice: How Emerging Democracies Reckon with Former Regimes* (Washington, D.C.: United States Institute of

Peace Press, 1995); several articles by independent researcher Priscilla Hayner, including: "Fifteen Truth Commissions—1974 to 1994: A Comparative Study," *Human Rights Quarterly* 16, no. 4 (1994): 598–655, "Commissioning the Truth: Further Research Questions," *Third World Quarterly* 17, no. 1 (1996): 19–29, and "International Guidelines for the Creation and Operation of Truth Commissions: A Preliminary Proposal," *Law and Contemporary Problems* 59, no. 4 (autumn 1996): 173–180 (Hayner also has a book forthcoming on these questions); Aryeh Neier, *War Crimes: Brutality, Genocide, Terror, and the Struggle for Justice* (New York: Times Books, 1998); and Martha Minow, *Between Vengeance and Forgiveness: Facing History after Genocide and Mass Violence* (Boston: Beacon Press, 1998). On the South African TRC in particular, see Kader Asmal, Louise Asmal, and Ronald Suresh Roberts, *Reconciliation through Truth: A Reckoning of Apartheid's Criminal Governance*, 2d ed. (New York: St. Martin's Press, 1997); Antjie Krog, *Country of My Skull* (Johannesburg: Random House, 1998); Paul Van Zyl, "Dilemmas of Transitional Justice: The Case of South Africa's Truth and Reconciliation Commission," *Journal of International Affairs* 52, no. 2 (spring 1999): 647–667; a series of monographs published by the Centre for the Study of Violence and Reconciliation in Johannesburg, South Africa; Timothy Garton Ash, "True Confessions," *New York Review of Books*, July 17, 1997, 33–38; and Lyn S. Graybill, "Pursuit of Truth and Reconciliation in South Africa," *Africa Today* 45, no. 1 (1998): 103–134.

6. See Hayner, "Fifteen Truth Commissions," as well as her subsequent work.

7. See The National Unity and Reconciliation Act, Act No. 34, 1995, Republic of South Africa, *Government Gazette*, vol. 361, no. 16579 (Cape Town: July 26, 1995). Hereafter referred to in these notes as "the Act."

8. I also made this argument in "TRC Is a Prayer for South Africa's Future," *Star*, March 11, 1999; an unedited version was also carried in the *Pretoria News* on the same date. See also Hayner, "Commissioning the Truth: Further Research Questions," 19–28. As Hayner points out, "truth commissions can sometimes be set up as a whitewash, projecting the image of a concern for human rights, satisfying the donors who provide aid, but representing no will to change."

9. General Pinochet was held under house arrest in the United Kingdom for a year and a half while his extradition case worked its way through the British justice system. In March 2000, he was allowed to return to Chile, after British home secretary Jack Straw determined that the ailing Pinochet was not fit to stand trial. In August, the Chilean Supreme Court lifted Pinochet's senatorial immunity, but it remains to be seen whether the general will be brought to trial.

10. The Statute of the International Criminal Court does not empower the future court to hear cases that predate the entry into force of the 1998

Rome Treaty (this will occur only after sixty countries have ratified the treaty; as of September 2000, nineteen countries have done so). Therefore, the amnesties that cover acts that took place between 1960 and 1994 are not threatened by this particular form of external intervention. The extradition scenario represented by the Pinochet case does, however, present a credible threat to South African perpetrators. See John Dugard, "Dealing with Crimes of a Past Regime: Is Amnesty Still an Option?" (the Third Manfred Lachs Memorial Lecture, delivered at "The TRC: Commissioning the Past," a conference cohosted by the History Workshop, University of the Witwatersrand, and the Centre for the Study of Violence and Reconciliation, June 11–14, 1999).

11. See Hayner, "International Guidelines." Hayner builds on suggested guidelines in the reports of Special Rapporteur Louis Joinet to the United Nations Commission on Human Rights Sub-Commission on Prevention of Discrimination and Protection of Minorities (E/CN.4/Sub.2/1996/18, E/CN.4/Sub.2/1997/20).

12. Final Report, 1:5, par. 100, p. 131.

2. THE BENEFITS OF LEARNING FROM OTHERS' MISTAKES

1. Timothy Garton Ash, "The Truth about Dictatorship," *New York Review of Books*, February 19, 1998, 36.

2. There is a wealth of literature on the negotiations that led to multiparty democracy in South Africa. See, for example, Patti Waldmeir, *Anatomy of a Miracle: The End of Apartheid and the Birth of the New South Africa* (New York: W. W. Norton, 1997); and Alistair Sparks, *Tomorrow Is Another Country: The Inside Story of South Africa's Road to Change* (Chicago: University of Chicago Press, 1996). See also Peter Parker, "The Politics of Indemnities, Truth Telling, and Reconciliation in South Africa: Ending Apartheid without Forgetting," *Human Rights Law Journal* 17, nos. 1–2 (April 30, 1996): 1–12.

3. Ash, "Truth about Dictatorship," 36. Ash does not give a citation for the Rosenberg quotation, but Rosenberg's analysis would be familiar to South African participants in the conference organized by the Institute for Democracy in South Africa (IDASA) (see note 8) at which she participated.

4. Ibid.

5. See Final Report, 5:6, pars. 126–129, pp. 237–239.

6. Kader Asmal, "Fears and Hopes," in *The Healing of a Nation?* ed. Alex Boraine and Janet Levy (Cape Town: Justice in Transition, 1995), 27.

7. Graeme Simpson, *Proposed Legislation on Amnesty/Indemnity and the Establishment of a Truth and Reconciliation Commission* (Johannesburg: CSVR, 1994), 12, a submission made in June 1994 on behalf of the Centre for the Study of Violence and Reconciliation to Minister of Justice Dullah Omar.

8. In 1992, IDASA sponsored a group of South Africans to visit several central European countries to observe the issues confronting those societies in transition from totalitarianism to democracy. In 1994, IDASA and Justice in Transition organized two conferences that brought together delegates from countries ranging from Argentina and Chile to Bulgaria and Germany, along with journalists, academics, and opinion leaders, to reflect on the experiences other countries had with transitional justice issues and possible implications for South Africa. See the conference proceedings, Alex Boraine, Janet Levy, and Ronel Scheffer, eds., *Dealing with the Past: Truth and Reconciliation in South Africa* (Cape Town: IDASA, 1994); and Boraine and Levy, eds., *Healing of a Nation?*

9. For an assessment of the overall role of NGOs in the TRC process, see Hugo van der Merwe, Polly Dewhirst, and Brandon Hamber, "The Relationship between Peace/Conflict Resolution Organisations and the Truth and Reconciliation Commission: An Impact Assessment" (paper prepared for the International Study of Peace Organisations—SA, a conference funded by the Aspen Institute, October 7, 1998). The authors point out that representatives of some NGOs felt marginalized from this process.

10. Alex Boraine, interview by author, New York, February 3, 1999.

11. In addition to citing Boraine, van der Merwe, Dewhirst, and Hamber also mention C. A. Norgaard (European Commission on Human Rights), Andre du Toit (University of Cape Town), Arthur Chaskalson and Albie Sachs (both of whom were subsequently appointed to the Constitutional Court), John Dugard (University of the Witwatersrand), Lourens du Plessis (University of Stellenbosch), and George Bizos and Mohamed Nasvat (both of the Legal Resources Center) as playing important roles in the drafting process ("Relationship between Peace/Conflict Resolution Organisations and the Truth and Reconciliation Commission," 5).

12. African National Congress National Executive Committee's Response to the Motsuenyane Commission's Report, August 29, 1993.

13. Ibid., 6. See also Johannes Rantete, *The African National Congress and the Negotiated Settlement in South Africa* (Pretoria: J. L. van Schaik/Academic, 1998), 64; and Final Report, 1:4, pars. 6–7, pp. 49–50.

14. Willie Hofmeyr, interview by author, Cape Town, December 5, 1998. See also Van Zyl, "Dilemmas." Reflecting the ANC's mindfulness of the NP's position, Van Zyl (p. 650) quotes Dullah Omar, a key ANC negotiator and former minister of justice, as stating that "without an amnesty agreement there would have been no elections."

15. Specifically, the ANC sought to achieve a moral balance by conditioning individual amnesties on full disclosure, which would, on the one hand, help meet the victims' need for truth and, on the other hand, offer victims a platform to tell their stories, along with some sort of reparations.

16. Under the heading "National Unity and Reconciliation," the postamble reads:

This Constitution provides a historic bridge between the past of a deeply divided society characterised by strife, conflict, untold suffering and injustice, and a future founded on the recognition of human rights, democracy and peaceful co-existence and development opportunities for all South Africans, irrespective of colour, race, class, belief or sex.

The pursuit of national unity, the well-being of all South African citizens and peace require reconciliation between the people of South Africa and the reconstruction of society.

The adoption of this Constitution lays the secure foundation for the people of South Africa to transcend the divisions and strife of the past, which generated gross violations of human rights, the transgression of humanitarian principles in violent conflicts and a legacy of hatred, fear, guilt and revenge.

These can now be addressed on the basis that there is a need for understanding but not for vengeance, a need for reparation but not for retaliation, a need for ubuntu but not for victimisation.

In order to advance such reconciliation and reconstruction, amnesty shall be granted in respect of acts, omissions and offences associated with political objectives and committed in the course of the conflicts of the past. To this end, Parliament under this Constitution shall adopt a law determining a firm cut-off date, which shall be a date after 8 October 1990 and before 6 December 1993, and providing for the mechanisms, criteria and procedures, including tribunals, if any, through which such amnesty shall be dealt with at any time after the law has been passed.

With this Constitution and these commitments we, the people of South Africa, open a new chapter in the history of our country.

Nkosi sikelel' iAfrika. God seen Suid-Afrika

Morena boloka sechaba sa heso. May God bless our country

Mudzimu fhatutshedza Afrika. Hosi katekisa Afrika

17. There are a number of recently published or forthcoming books on the TRC. See, for example, Desmond Tutu Mpilo, *No Future without Forgiveness* (New York: Doubleday, 1999). In addition, TRC deputy chairperson Alex Boraine is expected to publish an account of the TRC process in October 2000. Priscilla Hayner's forthcoming book on truth commissions will also address the TRC in comparative context.

18. Jose Zalaquett, "Why Deal with the Past?" in Boraine, Levy, and Scheffer, *Dealing with the Past*, 11.

19. Final Report, 1:4, par. 25, p. 54.

20. Minow, *Between Vengeance and Forgiveness*, 57.

21. Eligibility and criteria for granting amnesty are spelled out in Section 20 (1), (2), (3), and (4) of the Act. In determining whether an act meets the definition of having a political objective, the Amnesty Committee would weigh several criteria, including the applicant's motive, the context in which the act took place, whether the act was committed at the behest of an organization, the nature of the act, the objective of the act, and the proportionality of the act with the political objective pursued. Parker ("Politics of Indemnities," 4–5) points out that the TRC's definition of political objective represents something of an amalgamation of the Norgaard principles (named for Carl Norgaard, president of the European Commission of Human Rights, who had been asked to advise on disputed cases concerning political violence in Namibia), along with the definitions used in both the 1990 Indemnity Act, which borrowed heavily from the Norgaard principles, and the 1992 Further Indemnity Act, which gave inordinate discretion to the state president.

22. Hofmeyr, interview.

23. Section 21 (2) stipulates that "if any criminal or civil proceedings were suspended pending a decision on an application for amnesty, and such application is refused, the court concerned shall be notified accordingly" but that "no adverse inference shall be drawn by the court concerned from the fact that the proceedings which were suspended pending a decision on an application for amnesty are subsequently resumed."

24. Graybill, "Pursuit of Truth and Reconciliation in South Africa," 118.

25. Amnesty Committee staff members, interviews by author, Cape Town, June 8, 1999. Although the TRC has given the NDPP a list of some one hundred perpetrators against whom it recommended prosecution, in the absence of a clear policy on this question, it is not clear how or when the NDPP will gain access to the supporting documentation in the TRC archives.

26. That said, some South African NGOs are currently undertaking to provide funding in support of lawsuits on behalf of victims of gross human rights violations who would otherwise be financially unable to bring civil claims against perpetrators whose identities are known and who either did not apply for, or did not receive, amnesty.

27 De Kock applied for amnesty for these crimes in March 1996. At the time of the writing of this book, he had received amnesty for some incidents—including for his involvement in the May 7, 1987, bombing of COSATU House (occupied by the Congress of South African Trade Unions); the August 1988 bombing of Khotso House (which housed the South African Council of Churches); the June 27, 1985, murders of the "Cradock Four" (Matthew Goniwe, Sparrow Mkhonto, Fort Calata, and Sicelo Mhlauli); and the March 1982 bombing of the ANC offices in London.

He was refused amnesty in the "Motherwell" case, which concerns the December 14, 1989, murder of three members of the Port Elizabeth Security Police and one "askari" (a "turned" former liberation fighter), who was also affiliated with the Security Police. A number of other cases for which de Kock applied for amnesty remain outstanding.

28. See Eugene de Kock, as told to Jeremy Gordin, *A Long Night's Damage: Working for the Apartheid State* (Saxonwold: Contra Press, 1998).

29. Ash, "True Confessions," 38.

30. Max du Preez, "Blanket Amnesty: Act of Betrayal," *Sunday Independent*, November 8, 1998.

31. Jose Zalaquett, "Chile," in Boraine and Levy, *Healing of a Nation?* 52.

32. Simpson, "Proposed Legislation," 12.

33. Van Zyl, "Dilemmas," 652.

34. The Act, Section 4 (d).

35. Final Report, 1:11, par. 33, p. 332.

36. Piers Pigou, who was addressing a seminar organized by the Centre for the Study of Violence and Reconciliation, was quoted in "Truth Commission's Failed, Says a Former Star Investigator," *Electronic Mail and Guardian*, April 28, 1998.

37. In the context of multiparty talks leading to the Interim Constitution, the ANC, at the suggestion of Joe Slovo, leader of the SACP, agreed to a "sunset clause," which provided for apartheid-era functionaries to be given a grace period during which they would not be removed from office once the ANC-led government came to power.

38. John Daniel, remarks during a presentation at the conference, "The TRC: Commissioning the Past."

39. Dumisa Ntsebeza, interview by author, Cape Town, December 3, 1998.

40. Fazel Randera, interview by author, Pretoria, June 18, 1999.

41. Graeme Simpson, interview by author, Johannesburg, December 9, 1998.

42. The IFP subsequently backed down from this hard-line position, but its leaders' continuing public and vocal opposition to the TRC had the effect, in the words of the Final Report (5:6, par. 23, p. 200) of "dissuading thousands of ordinary IFP supporters from coming forward to the Commission." Few IFP members applied for amnesty.

43. P. W. Botha submitted seventeen hundred pages of written responses to questions posed by the TRC, but he refused to appear in person at the TRC's hearing, in defiance of a subpoena directing him to do so, and in spite of personal interventions by both Tutu and Mandela. The TRC had sought to question Botha about evidence given in the course of several amnesty hearings subsequent to his written submissions that implicated him in several state-sponsored atrocities. Botha was charged with contempt for defying the subpoena, but he got off on a technicality.

44. Final Report, 1:1, par. 80, p. 20.

45. Zalaquett, "Chile," 52.

46. The Act, Section 4 (a)(ii).

47. Paul Van Zyl, interview by author, New York, February 3, 1999.

48. Final Report, 1:6, par. 39, pp. 148–149.

49. Van Zyl, interview.

50. Final Report, 4:4, pars. 44 (c) and 48, pp. 107–108.

51. Ibid., 4:2, p. 21. See also Final Report, 4:2, par. 11, p. 20 for Old Mutual's self-exemption.

52. From the ANC submission to the TRC, as cited in the Final Report, 4:2, par. 16, p. 22.

53. Two passive-voice recommendations are illustrative: "that consideration be given to the most appropriate ways in which to provide restitution for those who have suffered from the effects of apartheid discrimination" and that "the feasibility of the following as means of empowering the poor should be considered: a wealth tax; a once-off levy on corporate and private income; each company listed on the Johannesburg stock exchange to make a once-off donation of one percent of its market capitalization." Final Report, 5:8, par. 39, pp. 318–319.

54. Mahmood Mamdani criticized the TRC for its overemphasis on perpetrators and victims of gross human rights violations, while neglecting the enabling role of beneficiaries. See Mahmood Mamdani, "Reconciliation without Justice," *Southern African Political and Economic Monthly* 10, no. 6 (1997): 22–25. See also Mamdani's "A Diminished Truth," *Siyaya!* 1, no. 3 (spring 1998): 38–40. Mamdani praises the TRC for having discredited the apartheid regime in the eyes of its beneficiaries. But in doing so, he argues, the TRC failed to confront beneficiaries with their own culpability: "The TRC invited beneficiaries to join victims in a public outrage against perpetrators. If only we had known, it seemed to invite beneficiaries to say, we would have acted differently; our trust has been violated, betrayed, abused. . . . The more beneficiaries were outraged at gross violations, the less they felt responsible for them." See also Krog, *Country of My Skull*, 109–113. Drawing from a panel discussion at the University of Cape Town about reconciliation, Krog has written, "Where reconciliation for Tutu is the beginning of a transformative process . . . for Mbeki reconciliation is a step that can follow only after total transformation has taken place"; Mamdani "cuts the whole debate loose of the hazy black and white distinctions stifling most of the current thinking, by asking, 'If truth has replaced justice in South Africa—has reconciliation then turned into an embrace of evil?'" Contrasting South Africa's situation ("few perpetrators, but lots and lots of beneficiaries") with Rwanda ("a lot of perpetrators and a few people who benefited"), Mamdani asks "whether it is not easier to live with perpetrators than with beneficiaries?"

55. Krog, *Country of My Skull,* 113.

56. See Gunnar Theissen, *Between Acknowledgement and Ignorance: How White South Africans Have Dealt with the Apartheid Past* (Johannesburg: CSVR, 1997), a research report based on a CSVR public opinion survey conducted in March 1996. Theissen writes that "only few white South Africans feel that those people who supported the National Party in the past, have at least, to a certain degree, been responsible for the repression of black communities. Instead of reflecting their own participation in the former political system, the responsibility for the atrocities is mainly placed on the doorsteps of anti-apartheid activists and 'troublemakers' in black communities and to a lesser degree on the security forces and former NP governments" (p. 82). It is interesting to consider differences within the white population regarding their willingness to acknowledge responsibility for trying to undo the damage inflicted on the black community: "Female respondents were less eager to deny responsibility than their male counterparts and nearly twice as many English-speaking whites admitted responsibility compared to Afrikaans-speaking respondents. Respondents with post-matric education were more inclined to acknowledge than deny that the past regime and its executive organs were responsible. The younger generation (under the age of 30) were also far more likely to acknowledge responsibility" (p. 70).

3. THE POLITICS OF THE TRC

1. Michael P. Scharf, "Responding to Rwanda: Accountability Mechanisms in the Aftermath of Genocide," *Journal of International Affairs* 52, no. 2 (spring 1999): 626–627. Priscilla Hayner makes a similar argument in "Fifteen Truth Commissions."

2. That said, this argument should not be overstated, either. There is no evidence to suggest that the TRC played a significant role in how South Africans voted in their second democratic elections in 1999.

3. See Final Report, 1:12 (b), par. 36: "The IFP criticised commissioners, committee members and some staff members in [KwaZulu-Natal] throughout the process. From the time that the first hearing took place, when several deponents gave evidence of IFP involvement in violence, hostile accusations of bias were received by letter and in newspaper articles, many in the form of personal attacks on certain commissioners and committee members. . . . The IFP refused to take part in the process and, despite many approaches, the Commission in the region had very little success in changing its attitude. Representation at hearings was, therefore, inevitably skewed."

4. The Act, Section 7 (1) and (2)(a).

5. Ibid., Section 7 (2)(b). While such a requirement may reflect a laudable goal—that is, to preserve the integrity of the truth and reconciliation process by ensuring that the commission not become a vehicle for politically motivated actions—it strikes me as somewhat preposterous, in retrospect. Apartheid had a way of politicizing everything, and even among those commissioners who did not have a "high political profile," many were known to be affiliated with particular political institutions. Indeed, some of the commissioners, including the commission's chairperson, Mary Burton, a former president of the human rights organization Black Sash, were well-known activists. Certainly, if the commissioners did not have a high political profile going into the process, they came to have one in the course of their work with the TRC.

6. I base this observation on informal conversations and my own impressions of South Africa—having lived there in 1992–94 and having spent several months in the country in 1998–99. One can only speculate about the conspiracy theories that would have circulated had a foreigner or two—however well qualified—been included among the commissioners.

7. Two of the original seventeen commissioners stepped down midway through the process (Chris de Jager did so to serve on the Amnesty Committee). In addition to the seventeen, the Act provided for the appointment of committee members other than commissioners to serve on the Human Rights Violations and Reparation and Rehabilitation Committees. The TRC did appoint such members, both to provide these committees with needed assistance and to ensure that committee membership was representative in terms of race, gender, and geographical origin.

8. *Star*, October 26, 1998.

9. Van Zyl, interview.

10. Boraine, interview.

11. Ibid.

12. Tutu does refer to such tensions in his introduction to the Final Report, but he seems to indicate that they were more prevalent in the commission's early stages. See also Final Report, 1:4, par. 36, p. 58, for example: "In the process of interpreting the mandate, a number of difficult and often highly contested decisions had to be made." Of course, the fact that Commissioner Wynand Malan chose to submit a "Minority Position" also speaks volumes about these undercurrents.

13. These indemnifications, given without disclosing what the amnesties were for, as required in the Further Indemnity Act of 1992, were subsequently declared illegal. See Lourens Du Plessis, "Legal Analysis," in Boraine, Levy, and Scheffer, eds., *Dealing with the Past*, 108–112. See also Parker, "Politics of Indemnities."

14. The Act, Section 33.

15. The Act, Section 20 (1) spells out these criteria. Section 20 (2) and (3) explain how the Amnesty Committee is to determine whether or not an act was politically motivated.

16. Boraine, interview.

17. Graybill, "Pursuit of Truth and Reconciliation in South Africa," 117.

18. Interview by author. Although I cannot confirm that the paraphrased exchange took place, if one goes back to look at the press releases from the early amnesty decisions, one can imagine, more or less, when such an exchange might have occurred.

19. Charles Villa-Vicencio, interview by author, Cape Town, June 10, 1999.

20. Van Zyl, interview.

21. Ibid.

22. Randera, interview.

23. Ntsebeza, interview.

24. Van Zyl, interview.

25. See "Many in ANC Opposed to Asking for Amnesty, Says Mandela," *SAPA*, October 22, 1996.

26. Madikizela-Mandela insisted that she give testimony in public. The hearings lasted two weeks and ended on the eve of the 1997 ANC national congress, at which she was on the ballot as the ANCWL nominee for deputy president of the party. Madikizela-Mandela's supporters complained that the hearing was timed to damage her reputation and undermine her candidacy before the ANC congress. I found no evidence to support this claim; indeed, according to a number of TRC sources, had Madikizela-Mandela not insisted on public hearings, her case could have been heard much earlier. Clearly, ANC moderates used the negative publicity the hearings generated to further sideline the renegade Madikizela-Mandela within the party, even going so far, according to *New York Times* reporter Suzanne Daley, as to "dust off a little-noticed regulation that says the league [ANCWL] does not have the right to make nominations" ("Mrs. Mandela Gives Up Bid to Re-Ignite Political Career," *New York Times*, December 18, 1997). According to *Washington Post* reporter Lynne Duke, the "paltry show of hands in support of her nomination" resulted in Madikizela-Mandela withdrawing her candidacy ("Madikizela-Mandela Drops Bid for ANC No. 2 Post," *Washington Post*, December 18, 1997). The Final Report made severe findings against Madikizela-Mandela, finding that she had participated in assaults and abduction, that she had committed perjury, and that she was aware of several killings. Madikizela-Mandela did not apply for amnesty, but few observers expect her to be prosecuted. She had already been convicted in 1991 for her involvement in the Stompei Seipei kidnapping. Meanwhile, her political career has not completely withered: she appeared as number ten on the ANC's list of candidates for Parliament and she currently serves as an MP and continues in her post as president of the ANCWL.

27. Mathews Phosa, then ANC legal head, was left insisting that "the ANC did not grant itself amnesty and we did not apply for a blanket amnesty."

28. TRC statement, March 4, 1999.

29. "ANC Applications Did Not Comply with Law: TRC," *SAPA*, March 4, 1999.

30. Ibid.

31. *Cape Times*, April 28, 1999.

32. TRC statement, "Amnesty Denied to Hani Killers," April 7, 1999. See also "Accusations of Bias after White Extremists Refused Amnesty," *International Herald Tribune*, April 9, 1999; and "Demo against TRC Planned," *Cape Times*, April 30, 1999.

33. "Amnesties Not Even," *Citizen*, February 22, 1999. The editorial contrasts the Amnesty Committee's granting of amnesty to the "savages" who murdered the American Fulbright scholar Amy Biehl with the negative decision in the Biko case: "How can the murder of Amy Biehl be political while that of Steve Biko is not?" Considering that the *Citizen* has long been considered the newspaper of the (old and New) National Party (which insisted on some form of amnesty in the multiparty negotiations), it is somewhat ironic that the editorial goes on to argue that amnesties are "inherently wrong" for letting "wanton killers go free."

34. A TRC press release issued on December 9, 1999, summarizes the breakdown of amnesty decisions as of that date, per political affiliation. The numbers revealed no particular political bias, with amnesties granted and refused to members of all major political groupings. Amnesties were granted in 383 out of 552 cases to ANC members; amnesties for members of the security forces were granted in 124 cases out of 163.

35. Martin Coetzee, interview by author, Cape Town, December 1, 1998.

36. Ibid.

37. Final Report, 1:5, par. 63, p. 120.

38. Simpson, interview.

39. Van Zyl, interview.

40. The Act, Section 4 (f) and Section 27.

41. Final Report, 1:9, par. 45, pp. 253–254, and 5:5, par. 3, p. 170.

42. For an admittedly nonscientific sampling of victims' perspectives, see *Survivors' Perceptions of the Truth and Reconciliation Commission and Suggestions for the Final Report: Submission to the TRC*, compiled by the Centre for the Study of Violence and Reconciliation and the Khulumani Support Group (Johannesburg: CSVR, 1998). The vast majority of victims with whom I spoke expressed anger and frustration that their need for reparations—in addition to the moral imperative to provide reparations—was being ignored by the government.

43. Final Report, 5:5, par. 68, p. 184.

44. Ibid., 5:5, par. 75, p. 185.

45. See "ANC Cash Shock for Victims of Apartheid," *Sunday Times,* February 7, 1999.

46. "Mankahlana Denies Decision Made to Refuse Cash to Apartheid Victims," *SAPA,* February 7, 1999.

47. See http://www.anc.org.za/ancdocs/history/mbeki/1999/t0225.html.

48. Villa-Vincencio, interview.

49. Interview by author.

50. Van Zyl, interview.

51. Interview by author.

52. Van Zyl, "Dilemmas," 664.

53. Villa-Vicencio, interview.

54. Simpson, interview.

55. Hlengiwe Mkhize, interview by author, Cape Town, June 11, 1999. Also, see "Truth Commission 'Needs More Teeth,'" *Business Day,* April 22, 1998.

56. See Yasmin Sooka's keynote address to the conference, "The TRC: Commissioning the Past." Sooka expressed similar sentiments in an interview by the author, Johannesburg, June 11, 1999.

57. See TRC, *A Summary of Reparation and Rehabilitation Policy, Including Proposals to Be Considered by the President* (published by the TRC in 1998).

58. Khulumani has since organized marches to bring its message about reparations to the streets.

59. Although the text to this effect was redacted from the publicly released Final Report, the substance had been leaked to the press and is well known. See "What FW Did Not Want You to See," in *Mail & Guardian,* October 30–November 5, 1998. Many have made the point that by launching his court challenge, de Klerk stimulated greater public scrutiny of the TRC's findings. The same argument can be made with respect to the ANC's failed court bid.

60. The Cape High Court was to have issued a final decision on de Klerk's case in 1999, but de Klerk postponed the case. In the meantime, leaked minutes from a March 1984 State Security Council (SSC) meeting at which de Klerk was present have surfaced. According to the minutes, the SSC authorized the removal ("verwyder") of activist Matthew Goniwe. The delayed hearing of de Klerk's case may provide the TRC with the opportunity to question de Klerk about the minutes and his complicity in the murder of Goniwe.

61. "TRC Plan 'On Track,'" *Sowetan,* October 27, 1998.

62. "Submission of the African National Congress to the Truth and Reconciliation Commission in Reply to the Section 30 (2) of Act 34 of 1996 on the TRC 'Findings on the African National Congress,'" October 1998, par. 4.0.

63. See TRC statement, "Reaction to *Mail & Guardian* Article," October 9, 1998: "The reason for refusing the meeting is that we have laid down a procedure in terms of which all who receive Section 30 notices must respond by way of written representation. We have refused meetings to others who have asked for them. If we had a private meeting with the ANC over our findings, the inference could be drawn that we gave a liberation movement an unfair advantage over others. It would be a very sad day if the public were to develop the perception that we gave the ruling party such an advantage." Some observers have disputed the position that a face-to-face meeting between the TRC and the ANC would have been improper. See du Toit, "Perpetrator Findings as Artificial Even-Handedness? The TRC's Contested Judgments of Moral and Political Accountability for Gross Human Rights Violations" (unpublished paper on file with the author).

64. "ANC Clashes with Truth Commission over Final Report," *Electronic Mail & Guardian*, October 9, 1998.

65. Interview by author.

66. Interview by author.

67. "I Didn't Struggle against Tyranny to Substitute It," *Star*, October 30, 1998.

68. "Tutu Used His Casting Vote against ANC," *Sunday Independent*, November 1, 1998.

69. "ANC Blunders with TRC Interdict," *Mail & Guardian*, October 30–November 5, 1998.

70. "Mbeki 'Overruled' Mandela on TRC," *Saturday Star*, October 31, 1998.

71. This interpretation of the internal political dynamics is based on information from a number of the author's interviews.

72. "Mbeki 'Overruled' Mandela on TRC." See also "ANC Blunders with TRC Interdict," which highlights the fact that "the two party officials most closely involved with the issues raised in the TRC—Minister of Justice Dullah Omar and Mpumalanga premier Mathews Phosa, who heads both the ANC's legal department and its TRC unit—were only notified of the decision to take court action. Their opinion on the matter was not sought."

73. Interview by author.

74. Final Report, 5:8, par. 14, p. 309.

75. This comment was widely reported. See, for example, "Perpetrator-Friendly Politicians Are Threatening to Hold Justice to Ransom Again," *Sunday Independent*, November 8, 1998.

76. Ibid.

77. *Star*, November 11, 1999.

78. This was a common theme in several interviews I conducted with various South African political commentators.

79. See "Mandela on Evil, Amnesty, and the Death Sentence," *Sunday Independent*, December 6, 1998.

80. "Proposed Blanket Amnesty Worries Lawyers and Former TRC Staff," *Star*, May 26, 1999.

81. "Blanketing the Truth," *Business Day*, May 25, 1999.

82. See http://www.anc.org.za/ancdocs/history/mbeki/1999/tm0225.html.

83. "Amnesty Plan Sought for KwaZulu Natal," *Cape Argus*, February 26, 1999. Former justice minister Omar's remarks are paraphrased in the publication.

84. "Blanketing the Truth." While not a threat to the state, race relations within the SANDF remain volatile and potentially violent.

85. The adjectives "blanket," "general," and "collective" have been used quite interchangeably in the South African press to describe the amnesty mechanism apparently being contemplated by the South African government. As Jonathan Klaaren, professor of law at the University of the Witwatersrand, pointed out, there are important legal distinctions to consider: a blanket (or general) amnesty entails amnesty for certain acts for all people; a collective amnesty is where criminal liability for a certain class of persons is extinguished, where those acts fall within the terms of the legislation. Part of the problem, of course, is that no one yet knows what guise, if any, a post-TRC amnesty provision might take. Most observers believe the new initiative will be a *collective* amnesty. See Klaaren, "A Second Organizational Amnesty?" (paper presented at the conference, "Commissioning the Past").

86. See "TRC Sends Names to Prosecutor," *Cape Argus*, April 28, 1999. See also the TRC statement of the same date, in which the TRC confirms that it had "working discussions" with the NDPP's office and that a list was handed over. The TRC said that it would be inappropriate to discuss the names on the list or their exact number. See also Final Report, 5:8, par. 14, p. 309.

87. Amnesty Committee staff member, interview by author, Cape Town, June 8, 1999.

88. As this book went to press, the only case arising from the TRC process that has made it to trial is against Dr. Wouter Basson for his involvement in the apartheid government's chemical and biological weapons program.

4. REPORT CARD

1. Hayner, "International Guidelines," 173.

2. Ibid.

3. See the reports by Joinet (E/CN.4/Sub.2/1996/18 and E/CN.4/Sub.2/1997/20), which recommend fifty principles to combat impunity. Joinet's principles, which are unapologetically ambitious and leave no room to accommodate political constraints, are broken down into a right to know, a right to justice, and a right to reparations. Rather than endorsing the Joinet principles and/or proposing that the UN General Assembly adopt the principles, the Sub-Commission merely recommended that the Commission on Human Rights "establish follow-up machinery," thus effectively moving the principles to the back burner. See also the final report of UN Human Rights Commission special rapporteur Mo Cherif Bassiomni, "The Right to Restitution, Compensation, and Rehabilitation for Victims of Gross Violations of Human Rights and Fundamental Freedoms" (E/CN.4/2000/62).

In drawing from the Joinet principles, this paper confines itself to those principles that are concerned with extrajudicial commissions of inquiry. The underlying principle of a state's duty to prosecute human rights violations, which Joinet takes for granted under the "right to justice" rubric, would restrict states from granting amnesty for gross human rights violations. I leave it to others to debate this issue. See, for example, Diane F. Orentlicher, "Settling Accounts: The Duty to Prosecute Human Rights Violations of a Prior Regime," *Yale Law Journal* 100, no. 8 (June 1991). See also Yves Beigbeder, *Judging War Criminals: The Politics of International Justice* (New York: St. Martin's Press, 1999). Van Zyl frames the issue in refreshingly nonabsolutist terms: "One of the central criticisms of amnesty is that by preventing the prosecution and punishment of perpetrators, it removes the primary deterrent to criminal activity and therefore increases the likelihood of a recurrence of human rights abuse. The logic of this assertion collapses if . . . it is unlikely that perpetrators would be prosecuted successfully, even in the absence of an amnesty process" ("Dilemmas," 658). He goes on to note that "in agreeing to the amnesty, South Africa's leaders failed to comply with the obligation to punish perpetrators under international law. They did, however, attempt to minimize the most offensive features of amnesties by structuring the process so that it would help achieve the other obligations prescribed by international law" (pp. 661–662). Joinet's principles on reparations are as absolutist as those concerning justice. See also E/CN.4/1997/104, the appendix of which is a note by Theo van Boven, a former special rapporteur of the Sub-Commission, on the "Basic Principles and Guidelines on the Right to Reparation for Victims of (Gross) Violations of Human Rights and International Humanitarian Law," dated January 16, 1997.

4. The extent to which compliance with such minimal standards will be sufficient to stave off ICC intervention remains to be seen. Put crudely, is a passing grade (which the South African TRC would certainly merit) enough, or will the international community insist on an even higher standard? See Dugard, "Dealing with Crimes of a Past Regime," 13. Dugard argues that the prosecutorial discretion provided for in Article 53 (2)(c) of the Rome Treaty would allow ICC prosecutors to recognize domestic amnesties, and he suggests that guidelines drawn up for the exercise of prosecutorial discretion should address this thorny question. See also Neil J. Kritz,

"Coming to Terms with Atrocities: A Review of Accountability Mechanisms for Mass Violations of Human Rights," *Law and Contemporary Problems* 59, no. 4 (autumn 1996): 127–152. Kritz points out, among other things, that the ICC "will need to deal with the application of non-criminal sanctions in the context of the ICC's principle of complementarity. If a society reckons with its past demons through a non-prosecutorial accountability mechanism, such as administrative vetting and civil sanctions, should that preclude the international court from investigating and prosecuting the same cases?" (The South African model, it should be noted, does not even go this far.) Kritz continues: "Administrative penalties, after all, are not the same as impunity. Or should this be precisely the sort of situation that might trigger ICC involvement, given that national authorities may have settled for administrative measures because criminal prosecution was politically impossible? A framework needs to be developed to assist that assessment, because the issue will surely confront the ICC" (pp. 140–141). See also Final Report, 1:4, appendix A, par. 2. The TRC is explicit that, in sharing the international community's moral and legal position that apartheid was a crime against humanity, it is *not* calling for international criminal prosecution of those who formulated and implemented apartheid policies. "Indeed, such a course would militate against the very principles on which this Commission was established" (p. 94).

   5. The categories for evaluation that I use are drawn from those proposed by Hayner in "International Guidelines," in addition to the Joinet principles, which Hayner uses as her point of departure. Given the particularities of the South African model, I have taken the liberty of combining or otherwise modifying some of Hayner's and Joinet's principles, and I have dropped or downplayed elements from both. I try to indicate where assessments apply strictly to the TRC, to the government, to political parties, or to other actors; some can and should be applied across the board.

   6. Hayner, "International Guidelines," 178.

   7. Krog, *Country of My Skull,* 236–237.

   8. Hayner, "International Guidelines," 178.

   9. See van der Merwe et al., "Relationship between Peace/Conflict Resolution Organisations and the Truth and Reconciliation Commission," 13–19.

   10. Simpson, interview.

   11. Van der Merwe et al., "Relationship between Peace/Conflict Resolution Organisations and the Truth and Reconciliation Commission," 10.

   12. Ibid., 23.

   13. Ibid., 32.

   14. The Act, Section 44.

   15. Admittedly, the Web site may have been more of a benefit to international audiences than domestic. This author can speak only for herself: it was and remains a tremendous resource. An "alternative TRC" Web site (www.struth.org.za), also quite useful, has been spun off by the official site's webmaster. Although the TRC Web site no longer carries the text of the Final Report, it does provide links to other sites where users can access the Final Report electronically, free of charge. Juta publishing house, which was awarded an exclusive contract to disseminate the Final Report, does so for R750 (about $125) for a bound copy or the same amount for a one-year subscription to its electronic version—a prohibitive price for the average South African. The bound volumes are also now available in the United States for $250.

16. Final Report, 1:4, par. 4, p. 49.

17. See http://www.anc.org.za/ancdocs/history/mandela/1999/nmo225.html.

18. See Final Report, 5:8 (preamble), p. 304: "We request the President of South Africa to call a National Summit on Reconciliation, not only to consider the specific recommendations made by the Commission, but to ensure *maximum involvement by representatives of all sectors of our society* in the pursuit of reconciliation" (emphasis mine).

19. Polly Dewhirst, "Post-TRC Prosecutions: An Instrument to Reveal More Truth" (paper presented at the conference "The TRC: Commissioning the Past").

20. Final Report, 5:9, par. 32, p. 366. There were also requests that "the programme of exhumation be extended to neighboring and other foreign countries."

21. Hofmeyr, interview.

22. Interviews by author.

23. Hayner, "International Guidelines," 179.

24. The Act, Section 3 (1).

25. Ibid., Section 11.

26. See *Survivors' Perceptions of the Truth and Reconciliation Commission.*

27. Forced removals under apartheid are akin to what has come to be referred to as "ethnic cleansing" in other parts of the world. Between 1960 and 1982, some 3.5 million nonwhite South Africans were subjected to state-directed collective expulsions and forced to migrate, usually to remote and barren rural areas. See Asmal, Asmal, and Roberts, *Reconciliation through Truth*, 133–134.

28. Mamdani, "Diminished Truth," 40.

29. E/CN.4/Sub.2/1997/20, 17. While sympathetic to complaints about this shortcoming in the TRC's mandate, I can hardly fault the decision to observe the ex post facto principle, especially in light of time and resource constraints that necessitated some limitation of the TRC's terms of reference. In addition, aside from the TRC, South Africa has other mechanisms (e.g., the Land Claims Tribunal) in which other categories of victims (e.g., victims of forced removals) can find redress.

30. The Act, Section 3 (a).

31. Final Report, 1:2, pars. 45–46, pp. 34–35.

32. Ibid., 1:1, par. 65, p. 16.

33. Hayner, "International Guidelines," 179; See also E/CN.4/Sub.2/1997/20, 17.

34. The Act stipulates, in Section 36 (1), that "the Commission, its Commissioners and every member of its staff shall function without political or other bias or interference and shall be independent and separate from any party, government, administration or any other functionary or body directly or indirectly representing the interests of any such entity."

35. I base this judgment on comments to this effect made in numerous personal interviews with a variety of interlocutors affiliated with the TRC.

36. I heard this anecdote on two occasions from two different interlocutors—both of whom were there.

37. Information based on personal interviews.

38. This came much to the shock of the NGO representatives in question, the CSVR and the Khulumani ("Speak Out") Survivor Support Group, who considered themselves "on the same side" as the commission on many matters. A better strategy might have been for the TRC to let such demonstrators serve a "bad cop" role to reinforce their own "good cop" representations to Parliament on reparations.

39. Accusations of bias against the commission came from parties across the political spectrum.

40. Graeme Simpson, informal remarks made at the conference "The TRC: Commissioning the Past"

41. The Final Report's chapter "Concepts and Principles" (1:5, pars. 11–28, pp. 106–110) reflects an awareness of the fact that "reconciliation is both a goal and a process." Of course, there are different levels of reconciliation, involving individuals (victims, perpetrators, beneficiaries) and groups at the community level and within society at large. Similarly, there are different shades of meaning for the term, ranging from the absence of retaliatory violence to more theological interpretations incorporating the notion of forgiveness. See also Krog's textured writing on this subject, *Country of My Skull,* 109–113; and Wolfram Kistner, "Reconciliation in Dispute" (paper presented at the conference "The TRC: Commissioning the Past").

42. For example, in a 1996 statement entitled "The Truth Will Set You Free," the SACC anticipated that the TRC process would create the space "where the deeper process of forgiveness, confession, repentance, reparation, and reconciliation can take place."

43. The TRC process did see several extraordinary reconciliatory exchanges between victims and perpetrators, such as when family members of victims of the St. James Church massacre in 1993 sought a meeting with the killers and offered their forgiveness. For many, the public displays of catharsis, forgiveness, and reconciliation pointed to the TRC's potential as catalyst for national healing. Nonetheless, many observers, in addition to victims and victim organizations, criticized Tutu for trying to impose reconciliation, which not only revictimized the victims but also encumbered the TRC process with his Christian beliefs and morals.

44. The Act, Section 4 (e).

45. See Priscilla Hayner's remarks on "The Truth and Reconciliation Commission: The South African Experience," at the Woodstock Colloquium on Forgiveness in Conflict Resolution: Reality and Utility— The Experiences of the Truth Commissions, Washington, D.C., March 11, 1998. Indicative of this difference, the Argentine truth commission's report, unlike the South African Final Report, was a bestseller, as were a number of other reports from nongovernmental commissions of inquiry in Latin America (such as *Nunca Mas* in Brazil).

46. Max du Preez, "Value of the TRC Is in the Process: The Final Report Is Purely Academic," *Cape Argus*, July 28, 1999.

47. Krog, *Country of My Skull*, 88.

48. The Act, Section 3 (1)(a).

49. While it is the author's assessment that the report is not biased, it should be noted that there are those who criticize the TRC for putting a particular "spin" on the truth. See, for example, Anthea Jeffrey, *The Truth about the Truth Commission* (Johannesburg: SAIIR, 1999). Jeffrey, a consultant to the South African Institute for Race Relations, has suggested that "far from being strong on the truth, as the Commission has claimed, it has produced a report which distorts as much as discloses the truth" by "heap[ing] the blame for violence" on the former security forces, and in some cases the IFP, while "at the same time any possible culpability of the ANC is downplayed or ignored." (See "TRC Downplayed ANC Blame," *SAPA*, July 27, 1999.) Jeffrey also faulted the TRC for its overreliance on victim statements, 90 percent of which were not given under oath and most of which were subject only to a low level of corroboration, as the basis for making derogatory findings. A number of respected writers have attacked Jeffrey's own biases (as an apologist for the apartheid state and security forces), conclusions, and methodology. For example, Polly Dewhirst commented at the conference "The TRC: Commissioning the Past" that the majority of information that came out of the TRC and provided the basis for the TRC's findings was the result of the amnesty process, not the human rights violations hearings or investigations. Jeremy Sarkin, in "The Truth about the Truth about the Truth Commission," *Sunday Times*, August 1, 1999, challenges, among other things, Jeffery's assumption that TRC findings should be rejected because they contradict the findings of previous inquests, noting that "inquests were often misled by security force personnel."

He dismisses her book, which, "in the guise of an academic study on the TRC's report, simply repeats the propaganda that she and other apologists for the former regime have been promoting for years." See also du Preez, "Value of the TRC Is in the Process," which dismisses Jeffrey's analysis as "reactionary bitterness" from the "New Right."

50. Michael Ignatieff, "Articles of Faith," *Index on Censorship* 5 (1996): 113, as cited in Final Report, 1:5, par. 33, p. 111.

51. See du Toit, "Perpetrator Findings." A number of individuals so named, not surprisingly, have likewise expressed concern; some, such as Mangosuthu Buthelezi, have brought lawsuits against the TRC.

52. This was a recurring theme in the papers presented at the conference, "The TRC: Commissioning the Past." See, for example, Deborah Posel, "The TRC Report: What Kind of History? What Kind of Truth?"

53. One would hope that this shortcoming would be remedied by the government's permitting of free public access to the entire TRC archive, including internal policy memoranda.

54. See du Toit, "Perpetrator Findings."

55. Final Report 1:4, par. 70, p. 67.

56. In Mbeki's parliamentary address regarding the Final Report, he criticized the report's "unfortunate and gratuitous insults to the armed struggle." See also the October 1998 "Submission of the African National Congress to the Truth and Reconciliation Commission in Reply to the Section 30 (2) of Act 34 of 1996 on the TRC 'Findings on the African National Congress,'" in which the ANC makes the case that the TRC "grossly misdirected itself" in its findings on the ANC. For example, the ANC objected to the finding that it "acted callously and with disregard for the families of persons executed," and "that SDUs [Self-Defense Units] perpetrated gross violations of human rights as a result of 'a contest for political terrain.'"

57. These statistics are from both a TRC statement, December 9, 1999, and the author's interview with an Amnesty Committee staff member, Cape Town, June 8, 1999. Of the outstanding cases, almost all will need to be heard in a public hearing, a very time-consuming process.

58. Ibid. Interestingly, between May and December 1999, over fifty additional applications were withdrawn. This increase suggests that perhaps the perceived threat of prosecutions had indeed waned.

59. Final Report, 1:7, par. 1, p. 174. The Final Report goes on to vent, "During its lifetime, the Commission was so often involved in litigation that one could be forgiven for thinking that it was under siege."

60. Jeremy Sarkin, "The Trials and Tribulations of South Africa's Truth and Reconciliation Commission," *South African Journal on Human Rights* 12, no. 4 (1996): 625.

61. Coetzee, interview. The high volume of amnesty applications is partly explained by the fact that those who were incarcerated—for any reason—had nothing to lose by applying. According to Coetzee, approximately 85 percent of the amnesty applicants were incarcerated.

62. "Truth Commission's Failed, Says a Former Star Investigator," *Electronic Mail & Guardian*, April 28, 1998.

63. Asmal, Asmal, and Roberts, *Reconciliation through Truth*, 17, 23.

64. See transcript from Craig Williamson's amnesty hearing, November 5, 1998.

65. Krog, *Country of My Skull*, 23.

66. The Act, Section 4 (f) and (h).

67. In addition to E/CN.4/Sub.2/1997/20, see former special rapporteur Theo van Boven's "Study Concerning the Right to Restitution, Compensation, and Rehabilitation for Victims of Gross Violations of Human Rights and Fundamental Freedoms," in E/CN.4/Sub.2/1993/8.

68. E/CN.4/Sub.2/1997/20, p. 25.

69. Final Report, 1:5, par. 93, p. 129.

70. E/CN.4/Sub.2/1997/20, p. 26.

71. See Final Report, 5:9, pars. 30–32, pp. 365–366, which details one such case, in which the TRC exhumed the remains of Phila Portia Ndwandwe (MK alias, Zandile), former acting commander of Natal MK activities initiated from Swaziland. "She was abducted from Swaziland by members of the Durban Security Branch but refused to cooperate with the police. It seems that the police did not have admissible evidence against her, but they felt they could not release her. She was kept in custody and tortured. Eventually she was killed and secretly buried on a farm in the Elandskop area, near Pietermaritzburg. When she was exhumed, her pelvic bones were covered with a plastic supermarket packet with which she had tried to protect the dignity of her naked body."

72. Many of the recommendations are grouped together under subject headings in 115 paragraphs. See Final Report, 5:8, pp. 304–349.

73. Ibid., 5:8, par. 24, p. 313.

74. Ibid., 5:8, par. 16, p. 310. See also par. 31 at p. 315, which assigns "responsibility for developing and implementing these recommendations" but does not fully clarify the question, Who should "assist communities preparing to accept such persons back into their midst"? And how should they do so?

75. Ibid., 5:8, par. 56, p. 326.

76. Consider, for example, the contrast between a recommendation regarding public order policing, which gives some context and rationale, and the nonrecommendation on lustration, which does not: "The police [should] be issued with new equipment and apparel to improve their safety and protection—the more protected the police officials feel, the less likely they are to use force or act aggressively" versus

"The Commission decided not to recommend lustration because it was felt that it would be inappropriate in the South African context." See ibid., 5:8, par. 71, p. 331, and par. 19, p. 311.

77. Both Verne Harris, of the National Archives of South Africa, and John Daniel, former staff member of the TRC Research Division, made remarks to this effect at "The TRC: Commissioning the Past." See Final Report, 5:8, par. 103, p. 344.

78. Ibid., 5:8, par. 14, p. 309.

79. Neil Kritz made comments to this effect at an informal discussion at the United States Institute of Peace on May 18, 1999, at which a draft of this paper was discussed. The author shares his concern and indeed raised it with a number of South African interlocutors. It should be noted, however, that not all scholars of truth commissions agree with his conjecture. Even if future truth commissions adopt the South African model, it can be argued, domestic circumstances would likely trump the South African experience.

80. That said, when confronted with this argument against blanket or group amnesties, most of my South African interlocutors, including those who hold policymaking positions, acknowledged this potential liability.

81. Final Report, 5:8, par. 33, p. 316.

82. Hayner, "International Guidelines," 178–179.

83. These numbers are from Hayner's remarks at the Woodstock Colloquium, 58, in addition to the author's conversations with staff members of the TRC and the Guatemalan commission.

84. See Final Report, 1:11, pars. 38–42, p. 300, and appendix, pp. 301–318.

85. Hayner's remarks at the Woodstock Colloquium, 58.

86. Final Report, 1:6, par. 4, p. 137.

87. Coetzee, interview.

88. Randera, interview.

89. Commissioners were anxious to capitalize on the goodwill associated with the country's first democratically elected government, but this goodwill was fast disintegrating. In fact, the NP withdrew from the GNU shortly after the commissioners were appointed.

90. TRC staff member, interview by author.

91. TRC commissioner, interview by author.

92. TRC staff member, interview by author.

93. Ibid.

94. Krog, *Country of My Skull*, 152.

95. Ibid., 153.

96. Zalaquett, "Chile," 51.

97. Hayner, "International Guidelines," 179–180.

98. Final Report, 1:11, par. 38, p. 300.

99. Randera, interview.

100. Suzanne Daley, "South African Panel's Report Arrives in Swirl of Bitterness," *New York Times*, October 30, 1998. Although some party representatives did attempt to manipulate public perceptions about the TRC to win votes in South Africa's second national elections in May 1999, the reality was that other hot-button issues such as crime, corruption, and the delivery of housing, electricity, and water to impoverished communities dominated public debates and discourse surrounding the elections.

101. E/CN.4/Sub.2/1997/20, 18.

102. See, for example, Anthea Jeffrey, "Can We Trust TRC Findings?" *Cape Times*, July 27, 1999. Jeffrey bemoans the fact that the TRC's "low level" of corroboration did not include corroborating the identity of perpetrators.

103. The Act, Section 30 (2).

104. Sarkin, "Trials and Tribulations," 638.

105. The Act, Section 21.

106. E/CN.4/Sub.2/1997/20, 18.

107. The Act, Section 35.

108. Final Report, 1:11 (Witness Protection Programme), par. 14, p. 390.

109. Final Report, 1:11 (Witness Protection Programme), par. 18, pp. 390–391.

5. EXTRAPOLATING FROM THE TRC

1. Of course, just because a truth commission is being contemplated does not mean one will be created. That said, there are ongoing discussions in several different parts of the world about the feasibility and appropriateness of truth commissions. For example, Sierra Leone's June 1999 Lome Peace Accord included provisions both for a blanket amnesty and for a truth and reconciliation commission, and in February 2000 Sierra Leone's Parliament approved TRC legislation. In addition, the government of Indonesia is considering establishing a commission. For some time, there have been discussions about a truth commission in Bosnia that would complement the work of the International Criminal Tribunal for the Former Yugoslavia. In the aftermath of the arrest of former Chilean dictator General Pinochet, some Chileans began calling for a more thorough accounting of their past. According to Priscilla Hayner (in an informal telephone conversation with the author in May 1999), other countries where either governmental representatives or NGOs have called for the establishment of a truth commission include Nigeria, Lesotho, Peru, and Colombia, though in each of these a commission would likely take a very different shape, if it comes into existence at all. Although there may be some proponents of a truth commission for Northern Ireland, the 1998 Good Friday Agreement purposefully excluded any such provision. Similarly, while there are proponents for some kind of truth commission for Cambodia and Rwanda, neither country is likely to be "ripe" for a truth commission in the near term.

2. Boraine, interview.

3. Final Report, 4:4, pars. 32–33, p. 101.

4. Desmond Tutu, speech delivered at a benefit for St. Barnabas College, Washington, D.C., May 14, 1999.

5. The Act, Section 3 (1).

6. In addition to Diane Orentlicher's "Settling Accounts" and Aryeh Neier's *War Crimes*, see *Law and Contemporary Problems* 59, no. 4 (autumn 1996), which is devoted to questions of "Accountability for International Crime and Serious Violations of Fundamental Human Rights." See also Van Zyl, "Dilemmas," for a well-argued defense of the TRC approach.

7. Final Report, 1:7, par. 1, p. 174.

8. For a summary of the Constitutional Court's decision in this case, see ibid., 1:7, pars. 10–11, p. 176. See also Sarkin, "Trials and Tribulations," 625–631. It is worth noting that the Constitutional Court's decision also takes note of the government's responsibility to pay reparations to victims. See the judgment of *Azanian People's Organisation v The President of the Republic of South Africa,* July 25, 1996: "Reparations are usually payable by states, and there is no reason to doubt that the postcript envisages our own state shouldering the national responsibility for those. It therefore does not contemplate that the state will go scot free. On the contrary, I believe, an actual commitment on the point is implicit in its terms, a commitment in principle to the assumption by the state of the burden." Following their loss before the Constitutional Court, the Biko family at least may still get justice. Those who had sought amnesty for killing Steve Biko were denied amnesty on grounds that the killing appeared to have been actuated by ill will or spite, rather than being politically motivated. In addition, the Amnesty Committee found that the applicants had conspired to conceal the truth and thereby failed to fully disclose the facts associated with their crime. The three individuals who sought amnesty for the killing of Griffiths Mxenge, for which they were previously charged and convicted, did receive amnesty, however.

9. Charles Villa-Vicencio drew the following analogy regarding the fear of justice as a motivator: "The threat of prosecutions is to the TRC what ICC intervention will be to future truth commissions." He opined that guidelines for determining whether the ICC should intervene should allow for amnesty in the context of full disclosure in public, with the threat of prosecution for those who do not come forward, but should expressly disallow "general amnesty." A general amnesty, he said, would "undermine a very, very, credible alternative to the ICC" (Villa-Vicencio, interview).

10. Final Report, 5:6, par. 101, pp. 222–223.

11. See "Submission of the African National Congress to the Truth and Reconciliation Commission in Reply to the Section 30 (2) of Act 34 of 1996." See also papers from the TRC's just war debate, which are posted on the TRC's Web site: www.truth.org.za. Several scholars of just war theory have pointed out an important distinction between *jus ad bellum* (justice of war) and *jus in bello* (justice in war). In lay terms, the ends do not justify the means in war. Thus, just war doctrine would dictate that, while the struggle to end apartheid was just, the actions of the liberation movements in this struggle are not automatically considered just; they would have to be weighed against *jus in bello* principles, including the protection of noncombatants, proportionality, and last resort. Interestingly, many amnesty applicants who had been agents of the apartheid state indicated that they, too—at least at the time the acts were committed—believed they had been fighting a "just war" against communism, terrorism, or anarchy.

12. Final Report, 1:1, par. 55, p. 13.

13. Commissioner Sooka indicated that the TRC had considered such a proposal, but that it was deemed to be inappropriate in the South African context, where the notion of "preferences" carried too much baggage from the apartheid years, when an array of benefits were distributed according to racial preferences (Sooka, interview).

14. Mkhize, interview. The TRC also considered a means test but rejected the idea because approximately 95 percent of victims were "ordinary people," and the cost of paying professional staff to weed out the other 5 percent would outweigh the savings.

15. In explaining the rationale behind its "victim findings," the Final Report (1:4, par. 82, p. 71) emphasizes the difference between the commission and a court of law, where "the full array of legal technicalities and nuances" might prohibit some victims from claiming compensation for their losses. This, the report states, would deviate from "the underlying objective of the legislators . . . to make it possible for the Commission to recognise and acknowledge as many people as possible as victims of the past political conflict."

16. See du Toit, "Perpetrator Findings," for a critique of the extent to which the TRC process was dominated by its perceived imperative to make perpetrator findings.

6. CONCLUSION

1. Richard Goldstone, interview by author, Johannesburg, November 13, 1998.

2. Zalaquett, "Why Deal with the Past?" 15. At the time of writing this book, the danger of backsliding, about which Zalaquett warned, appears pertinent in South Africa. Specifically, the ideal of no self-amnesty—a pillar upon which the ANC negotiated for the TRC—may, ironically, be imperiled, if indeed the ANC is contemplating a post-TRC collective amnesty that would cover, among others, itself, as an organization, in addition to thirty-seven of its leaders and many midlevel operatives whose earlier amnesties were overturned (for noncompliance with the full disclosure requirement of the act). In addition, if (as recent statements seem to indicate is likely) the government reneges on individual monetary reparations grants for victims of gross human rights violations, relying instead on symbolic, community-based reparations, the moral balance that the ANC sought to bring to the amnesty equation would be further eroded.

Dorothy Shea is a career foreign service officer. She served in South Africa from 1992 to 1994. She has also served as the Nigerian desk officer and as a member of the Policy Planning Staff of the U.S. Department of State. As the recipient of an International Affairs Fellowship from the Council on Foreign Relations, in 1998–99 she lectured at the University of the Witwatersrand in Johannesburg, South Africa, and was a guest scholar at the United States Institute of Peace. After completing this study, she returned to the State Department to work in the Office of War Crimes Issues. In September 2000, she became director for Multilateral and Humanitarian Affairs at the National Security Council.

JENNINGS RANDOLPH PROGRAM FOR INTERNATIONAL PEACE

This book is a fine example of the work produced by senior fellows in the Jennings Randolph fellowship program of the United States Institute of Peace. As part of the statute establishing the Institute, Congress envisioned a program that would appoint "scholars and leaders of peace from the United States and abroad to pursue scholarly inquiry and other appropriate forms of communication on international peace and conflict resolution." The program was named after Senator Jennings Randolph of West Virginia, whose efforts over four decades helped to establish the Institute.

Since 1987, the Jennings Randolph Program has played a key role in the Institute's effort to build a national center of research, dialogue, and education on critical problems of conflict and peace. Nearly two hundred senior fellows from some thirty nations have carried out projects on the sources and nature of violent international conflict and the ways such conflict can be peacefully managed or resolved. Fellows come from a wide variety of academic and other professional backgrounds. They conduct research at the Institute and participate in the Institute's outreach activities to policymakers, the academic community, and the American public.

Each year approximately fifteen senior fellows are in residence at the Institute. Fellowship recipients are selected by the Institute's board of directors in a competitive process. For further information on the program, or to receive an application form, please contact the program staff at (202) 457-1700 or visit the Institute's Web site, www.usip.org.

Joseph Klaits
Director